NEW KINGDOM FOCUSED GLOBAL MINISTRIES

Loving Singleness with Christ

A 52 Day Journey for Personal Growth

D1521658

"So the wall was completed in fifty-two days, on the twenty-fifth of Elul. When all our enemies heard about this, all the surrounding nations were afraid and disheartened, for they realized that this task had been accomplished by our God."

Nehemiah 6:15-16 (ESV)

Contents

Foreword

From the moment I heard about the vision for New Kingdom Marriage, I was gripped. At a time when it seems that so many people, especially women, face all sorts of difficulties in their personal relationships and often struggle to find Godly, suitable husbands, the New Kingdom Marriage group was creating a space to talk about real issues affecting both single and married people. This included the challenge of finding a Godly husband or wife, moving beyond past hurts and disappointments, and the desire to enter a divinely appointed marriage that would be loving, empowering, and enduring.

When New Kingdom Marriage first launched online, I often sat in the audience of the New Kingdom Marriage talks, listening to this amazing group of women discuss their future hopes and past experiences, contemplating their conversations and counsel, laughing with them at their personal challenges and considering the significance of this safe place they had succeeded in creating. It seemed to be a unique environment where people could be real and share about the highs and lows of relationships, discuss past hurts and traumas, share and receive guidance from both single and married people, and ultimately explore how singles might more effectively prepare themselves for Godly Christian marriage.

As these beautiful, confident women opened up about their experiences, sharing stories and lessons from choices that had either positively or negatively shaped their former relationships, transparently revealing the joys and disappointments each of them had encountered while navigating dating and courtship, I saw friendships forming, wisdom being shared, and assumptions about marriage being lovingly challenged. From communication to infidelity and submission to sexuality, these women explored topics that challenged us to examine our own issues and vulnerabilities. At the same time, they succeeded in injecting genuine love, concern, and humor into each conversation, each person gently nudging the other to reflect upon their own blind spots and, where needed, reconsider their views and assumptions about the many relationship scenarios they discussed.

Without question, with over a third of all marriages ending in divorce both in and outside of the church, there must be a more effective way to approach relationships and forge effective marital partnerships. Too often, individuals enter marriages with great expectations of what they should receive but a lesser understanding of what they need to give. In addition, there is often little consideration of each person's marital goals, whether these goals are aligned with their partner's goals, and how far each partner is willing to adapt or compromise to respond to their partner's needs.

Looking ahead, we want to see more new marriages formed that are successful and lifelong, but this requires individuals to have given more consideration to the realities of life before and after marriage and to have a clearer sense of their identity and purpose in God as singles. We want to see people healed from past wounds, who have been restored in God, and who can enter relationships feeling whole and not carrying baggage from former relationships. We want singles to have taken time to think about what really matters and to have understood the implications of commitment, fidelity, family, and what it takes for a marital relationship to successfully last 'til death do us part'.

With this New Kingdom Marriage journal, our authors have taken the heart of their online conversations and their passion for seeing individuals come into wholesome marital relationships and translated it into a devotional that will enable you to build a deeper relationship with God, receive healing for your soul, and to better understand how to listen to the Lord during periods of dating and courtship. It will also enable you to consider the joy, challenges, and implications of having children or moving forward after divorce and, ideally, to embrace this journey of reflection before you say, 'I do.'

Each week's reflections will help you to identify the relationship issues that really matter, to distinguish between the priorities and the less important, the nice to haves and the deal breakers, and with the wisdom and leading of the Holy Spirit, help you to move your marriage goals from the idealistic to the realistic. This God-filtered perspective will provide a solid platform for approaching marriage and will equip you to enter a marriage that is loving, wholesome, and purposeful.

During this self-reflective devotional journey with New Kingdom Marriage, take time to really focus on God. Let the Holy Spirit speak to you through each scripture and meditation, and allow Him to prepare and position you for successful, God-ordained marriage as you do.

Ruth Gordon

Simply Wisdom

Ordinary Women. Extraordinary Dreams

Acknowledgments

This journal is lovingly dedicated to all the participants who joined us at Clubhouse (New Kingdom Marriage within Six Months), sharing their journeys, wisdom, and hearts. To all the ladies seeking to prepare for and embrace the beautiful covenant of marriage, may this journey guide you toward deeper self-reflection, growth, and alignment with God's purpose for your life.

NEW KINGDOM FOCUSED GLOBAL MINISTRIES

Presents

Loving Singleness with Christ: A 52 Day Journey for Personal Growth

by

Jakki Gilchrist, Chimene Castor and, CaJuana Capps-King

Introduction

How much growth can be achieved in 52 days? The answer is more than we can imagine when intentionally aligning our hearts and lives with God. The powerful story of Nehemiah inspired the decision to create a 52-day prayer journal. In New Kingdom Focused Ministries, we are reminded of Nehemiah's mission to rebuild the walls of Jerusalem in 52 days—a task that was not only monumental in its physical demands but deeply spiritual in its significance. Before he began, Nehemiah prayed, fasted, and sought God's direction for four months. Despite fierce opposition, threats, and mockery, Nehemiah and the people pressed forward, refusing to be distracted or discouraged. Their steadfastness and obedience to God's plan led to an extraordinary victory.

This journal is designed to guide you through your own 52-day journey of growth, healing, and preparation. Whether you are single, dating, divorced, a single parent, or serving in ministry, this journal is crafted to meet you where you are. Each section invites you to reflect on the unique challenges and blessings you face in your season of life. You may find that some days resonate deeply, while others seem less relevant—but I encourage you not to skip over any part. God may use these reflections to reveal something new to you or equip you to bless someone else. Like any other season, singleness can feel like a time of waiting or wondering, but it is also a time of purpose.

As a Christian, this season of singleness is an opportunity for personal growth, deepening your relationship with God, and preparing your heart for whatever He has next. It's a time to build strong foundations—not just for future relationships but for your walk with Christ, your ministry, and your life. Like Nehemiah, you will likely face opposition along the way—doubts, distractions, and the pressures of life may try to pull you away from the work God is doing in you. But through prayer, fasting, and consistency, you will experience growth and victory.

This journal will help you stay rooted in God's Word and aligned with His will as you navigate this season and seek His guidance for your future. Over these 52 days, you will walk through five key sections:

1. **Singleness** – Embracing this season and discovering its purpose
2. **Courtship and Engagement** – Building godly relationships based on love, trust, and mutual purpose.
3. **Dating with Children** – Navigating the challenges and joys of dating as a parent.
4. **Divorced, Separated, and Healed** – Finding healing, restoration, and strength after separation or divorce.
5. **Dating While in Ministry** – Balancing personal relationships and the call to serve in ministry.

Each day of the journal will offer Scripture, reflections, and practical activities to help you grow spiritually, emotionally, and relationally. We believe that by the end of this journey, you will experience the kind of growth Nehemiah witnessed—steady, strong, and victorious. Nehemiah declared, "I am doing a great work and cannot come down." Let this be your declaration, too. You are doing great work in building your life according to God's will. May this journal be a tool that helps you grow closer to Christ, deepen your faith, and walk boldly into the purpose He has for you.

One

Part I: Being Single

W e all know that your first true love is more than memorable. Most people mention their first love throughout life in some way or another. Have you ever thought how God should be that true first love in your life? Our commitment should be to God first, and everything else should follow. God was the first one to love us. Considering how to love God back should be a priority. Serving and spending time with the one you love comes easy. It is something you want to do with no pressure. God wants the same. He wants a relationship. Personal commitment and intimacy are what God longs for from each of us. He wants to be the center of life for each of us. Learning to love God in your singleness is the greatest preparation for loving your spouse.

For the one who is single, this season of life is an opportunity to fully embrace independence and self-discovery. It is a time to explore personal passions, develop a strong sense of self, and build a life centered around faith and obedience to God. Being single allows for a focused period of growth and spiritual development, where one can dedicate time to understanding God's purpose for one's life without the distractions that come with a romantic relationship. It's a time to cultivate a deep relationship with God, engage in community, and prepare for the potential future roles God has planned.

Scriptural Guidance:

1 Corinthians 7:32-34: *"I want you to be free from anxieties. The unmarried man is anxious about the things of the Lord how to please the Lord. But the married man is anxious about worldly things, how to please his wife, and his interests are divided."*

This scripture emphasizes the advantage of being single in terms of undivided devotion to God. As a single person, you have the freedom to focus on your relationship with God and serve Him wholeheartedly.

Jeremiah 29:11: *"For I know the plans I have for you, declares the Lord, plans for welfare and not for evil, to give you a future and a hope."*

This verse reassures singles that God has a specific plan and purpose for their lives. Trusting in God's timing and plan can bring peace and confidence during the single season.

Kingdom Focused Activities:

- **Deepening Faith:** *Engage in regular Bible study, prayer, and worship to grow closer to God and understand His will for your life.*
- **Serving Others:** *Use your time and talents to serve in your church and community, reflecting God's love and advancing His kingdom.*
- **Personal Development:** *Invest in personal growth through education, hobbies, and skills that align with your God-given passions and purpose.*

Two

DAY 1: Know Who You Are

2 Corinthians 5:21 (NIV) God made him who had no sin to be sin for us, so that in him we might become the righteousness of God.

My Understanding of This Journey

Oh, isn't it amazing to reflect on the depth of God's love as expressed in 2 Corinthians 5:21? It fills my heart with joy to know that through Christ, I have been made the righteousness of God. It's like receiving the most precious gift imaginable—the gift of a relationship with Jesus Christ. In my own journey, I've come to cherish this truth deeply. Understanding who I am in Christ has been transformative—it's the cornerstone of living authentically and joyfully. But it wasn't always easy. There were moments when I struggled to see myself as worthy of God's love and purpose. Yet, through His grace and the support of my faith community, I've learned to embrace the truth of my identity in Christ.

One of the most delightful aspects of this journey has been the exploration of my values, beliefs, and passions. It's like uncovering treasures within myself, discovering what truly matters and brings me alive. I've learned to ask myself those fundamental questions: What do I stand for? What principles guide my decisions and actions? It's a joyful process of self-discovery, where

I've found that honesty, kindness, and perseverance are at the core of who I am.

And oh, the passions and interests that light up my soul! Whether it's painting, writing, volunteering, or simply immersing myself in the beauty of nature, these activities are more than just hobbies—they're expressions of my authentic self. They bring me immense joy and fulfillment, reminding me of the unique gifts and talents that God has bestowed upon me. Furthermore, contemplating my beliefs about the world and my place in it has been a source of profound insight and revelation. Whether spiritual, philosophical, or rooted in personal experiences, these beliefs shape my perspective and influence my interactions with others. They remind me of the beautiful diversity of God's creation and my role within it.

Lesson Learned

Ultimately, this journey of self-discovery has been about aligning my life with who I truly am rather than conforming to external expectations or societal pressures. It's a journey filled with joy, authenticity, and the boundless love of God. And as I continue to walk in the light of His truth, I am reminded of the incredible privilege it is to be called the righteousness of God through Christ.

Reflection

Take time today to reflect on your true self. Who are you at your core? What values, beliefs, and passions define you? Authenticity means being honest with yourself and others about who you are. Write down your thoughts and any revelations you have about your identity.

Prayer

Dear Heavenly Father, We come before You with hearts full of gratitude and awe. We thank You for Your indescribable love and the profound sacrifice You made for us. As Your Word says, **"God made Him who had no sin to be sin for us, so that in Him we might become the righteousness of God."** We are humbled by this incredible truth.

Lord Jesus, we thank You for willingly taking our sins upon Yourself, enduring the cross, and paying the ultimate price for our redemption. You, who knew no sin, became sin for us so that we might be reconciled to the Father and live in the freedom of Your righteousness. Help us, Lord, to always remember the depth of Your love and the magnitude of Your sacrifice. Let this truth transform our lives, guiding us to live in a way that reflects Your righteousness and brings glory to Your name.

Holy Spirit, empower us to walk in this new identity as the righteousness of God. Strengthen us to resist sin, pursue holiness, and share the message of Your grace with others. May our lives be a testament to Your love and mercy.

We pray this in the name of Jesus Christ, our Savior and Redeemer. Amen.

Three

DAY 2: Love Yourself

C olossians 3:14 (ESV) And above all this put-on love, which binds everything together in perfect harmony.

1 Corinthians 13:13 (ESV) So now faith, hope, and love abide, these three; but the greatest of these is love.

John 15:13 (ESV) Greater love has no one than this, that someone lay down his life for his friends.

My Understanding of This Journey

In Colossians 3:14, we're reminded to put on love above all else, for it is the force that binds everything together in perfect harmony. What a beautiful notion—to wrap ourselves in the warmth of love, allowing it to weave through every aspect of our lives, bringing peace and unity. But, if I'm honest, learning to love myself hasn't always been easy. It's a journey filled with ups and downs, a path paved with moments of self-doubt and uncertainty. But as I walk this journey, I'm discovering that loving myself is not selfish or indulgent; it's a profound act of self-compassion rooted in my identity as a beloved child of God. It's about recognizing my inherent worth and treating myself with the same kindness and understanding that I extend to others. It's about fixing my eyes on Jesus Christ, the embodiment of love, and allowing His grace to permeate my being, guiding me toward a deeper understanding of self-love.

In 1 Corinthians 13:13, we're reminded that faith, hope, and love abide, but the greatest of these is love. As I meditate on this truth, I find myself drawn to reflect on how I can embody this love in my daily life. It's about being kingdom-focused, prioritizing God above all else, and allowing His love to flow through me, enriching my interactions with others and nurturing my own well-being. **I'm learning to carve out time for rest and relaxation and recognizing the importance of maintaining my mental and physical health.** I'm engaging in activities that bring me joy and fulfillment, whether it's losing myself in a good book, experimenting with new recipes in the kitchen, or simply taking a leisurely stroll in nature. And amidst it all, I'm setting healthy boundaries, practicing positive self-talk, and extending forgiveness to myself for past mistakes.

In John 15:13, we're reminded of the greatest love of all—that of laying down one's life for a friend. As I reflect on this profound sacrifice, I'm prompted to cherish the aspects of my life that bring me joy and meaning. It's about treasuring the moments spent with loved ones, finding purpose in my work, and delighting in the simple pleasures of daily life.

Lesson Learned

I'm embracing my uniqueness and celebrating the incredible person that I am. I'm adopting new habits that promote my well-being, pampering myself with acts of self-care, and honoring the quirks and talents that make me who I am. Because self-love is not a destination—it's a continuous journey of appreciation and nurture, a journey that I'm grateful to walk every day as a single person.

Reflection

Focus on self-love and appreciation. How do you show love to yourself? What aspects of your life do you cherish and why? List the things you love about yourself and your life. Consider ways to enhance your self-care routine and celebrate your uniqueness.

Prayer

Dear Heavenly Father, We come before You with hearts open to Your love and grace. We thank You for the gift of love, which is the foundation of our faith and the essence of Your nature.

Your Word reminds us in Colossians 3:14, "And above all this put-on love, which binds everything together in perfect harmony." Lord, help us to clothe ourselves in love, allowing it to be the binding force that brings unity and peace to our lives, relationships, and communities. May Your love be the guiding principle in all we do, leading us to act with compassion, kindness, and humility.

In 1 Corinthians 13:13, You tell us, "So now faith, hope, and love abide, these three; but the greatest of these is love." Father, we thank You for the enduring presence of faith, hope, and love in our lives. We pray that we may always prioritize love above all else, recognizing its power to transform hearts and bring us closer to You and one another.

And as we reflect on John 15:13, "Greater love has no one than this, that someone lay down his life for his friends," we are reminded of the ultimate sacrifice made by Your Son, Jesus Christ. Lord, we are eternally grateful for His selfless act of love, laying down His life so that we might be saved. Help us to follow His example, loving others sacrificially and selflessly, and always putting their needs before our own.

Lord, fill us with Your love so that we may reflect Your heart in this world. Let our actions and words be a testament to Your love and grace. May we be instruments of Your peace, spreading love and harmony wherever we go.

We pray this in the name of Jesus Christ, our Savior and Redeemer. Amen.

Four

$\mathcal{DAY}$ 3: $\mathcal{Live}$ $\mathcal{Your}$ $\mathcal{Life}$

J **ohn 14:6 (ESV)** Jesus said to him, "I am the way, and the truth, and the life. No one comes to the Father except through me

John 3:16 (ESV) For God so loved the world, that he gave his only Son, that whoever believes in him should not perish but have eternal life.

John 6:35 (ESV) Jesus said to them, "I am the bread of life; whoever comes to me shall not hunger, and whoever believes in me shall never thirst.

Romans 6:23 (ESV) For the wages of sin is death, but the gift of God is eternal life in Christ Jesus our Lord.

John 10:10 (ESV) The thief comes only to steal and kill and destroy. I came that they may have life and have it abundantly.

My Understanding of This Journey

In John 14:6, Jesus declares, "I am the way, and the truth, and the life. No one comes to the Father except through me." This profound truth anchors my understanding of living a godly life. It's about embracing each day as a

11

gift, filled with endless opportunities to experience the abundance of God's love and grace. As I reflect on this verse, I'm reminded to approach each day with intention and enthusiasm, seeking to live life to the fullest in alignment with God's will. Living life to the fullest, for me, means embracing each moment with joy and purpose. It's about starting my day with a morning routine that sets a positive tone, filling it with activities that nourish my soul and bring me closer to God. Whether it's spending time in prayer and meditation, enjoying a nutritious breakfast, or going for a rejuvenating walk in nature, I strive to begin each day with gratitude and anticipation for what lies ahead.

In John 3:16, we're reminded of the depth of God's love for us: "For God so loved the world, that he gave his only Son, that whoever believes in him should not perish but have eternal life." This love is the foundation of my journey towards living a godly life, infusing each moment with joy and fulfillment. As I reflect on the activities that bring me true happiness, I'm reminded of the simple yet profound moments that make life worth living.

From engaging in creative pursuits to spending quality time with loved ones, each activity is an opportunity to experience God's abundant love and grace. Whether it's immersing myself in painting or writing, basking in the beauty of nature, or simply enjoying a meal with friends, these moments fill me with a sense of connection and purpose. They remind me of the abundant life that Jesus came to give us—a life filled with joy, peace, and fulfillment. In John 10:10, Jesus contrasts His purpose with that of the thief, stating, "The thief comes only to steal and kill and destroy. I came that they may have life and have it abundantly." Today, I choose to embrace this abundant life by intentionally planning a day filled with activities that bring me joy and fulfillment. From nurturing my passions to connecting with others, each moment is an opportunity to experience the richness of God's blessings.

Lesson Learned

As I reflect on my experiences at the end of the day, I'm filled with gratitude for the abundance of blessings in my life. These reflections serve as a reminder of the importance of living intentionally, embracing each moment with joy and purpose. By aligning my life with God's will and seeking to live in accordance with His love, I'm able to experience the fullness of life that Jesus promises—an abundant life overflowing with joy, peace, and love.

Reflection

Living your life to the fullest is essential. How do you make the most out of each day? What activities bring you joy and fulfillment? Plan a day filled with activities you love, and write about your experiences and how they contribute to your overall happiness.

Prayer

Dear Heavenly Father, We come before You with hearts full of gratitude and reverence. We thank You for Your boundless love and theprecious gift of Your Son, Jesus Christ. Lord Jesus, you declared in John 14:6, "I am the way, and the truth, and the life. No one comes to the Father except through me." We acknowledge that You are the only path to the Father, the ultimate truth, and the source of eternal life. Guide us in Your way, fill us with Your truth, and grant us the life that only You can give.

In John 3:16, we are reminded of Your incredible love: "For God so loved the world, that he gave his only Son, that whoever believes in him should not perish but have eternal life." Father, we are eternally grateful for this divine love and the promise of eternal life through belief in Your Son. Strengthen our faith and help us to live in a manner that reflects this profound gift.

Jesus, You also said in John 6:35, "I am the bread of life; whoever comes to me shall not hunger, and whoever believes in me shall never thirst." We come to You, seeking fulfillment and nourishment that only You can provide. Satisfy our spiritual hunger and quench our thirst with Your presence and Word.

As we consider Romans 6:23, "For the wages of sin is death, but the free gift of God is eternal life in Christ Jesus our Lord," we are reminded of the gravity of sin and the extraordinary grace You offer. Thank You for the gift of eternal life through Jesus Christ. Help us to turn away from sin and embrace the life You have given us.

Lastly, in John 10:10, You said, "The thief comes only to steal and kill and destroy. I came that they may have life and have it abundantly." We rejoice in the abundant life You provide, a life filled with purpose, peace, and joy. Protect us from the schemes of the enemy and lead us into the fullness of life that You have promised.

Lord, we are grateful for Your love, grace, and the eternal life we have in You. Help us to walk in Your way, live in Your truth, and embrace the abundant life You offer.

We pray this in the mighty name of Jesus Christ, our Savior and Redeemer. Amen.

Five

DAY 4: Walking in Your Ministry

Galatians 6:7-10 (ESV) Do not be deceived: God is not mocked, for whatever one sows, that will he also reap. For the one who sows to his own flesh will from the flesh reap corruption, but the one who sows to the Spirit will from the Spirit reap eternal life. And let us not grow weary of doing good, for in due season we will reap, if we do not give up. So then, as we have opportunity, let us do good to everyone, and especially to those who are of the household of faith.

Proverbs 16:3 (ESV) Commit your work to the Lord, and your plans will be established.

My Understanding of This Journey

Proverbs 16:3 reminds me to commit my work to the Lord, trusting that He will establish my plans. This verse serves as a guiding light on my journey, reminding me to surrender my ambitions and aspirations to God's loving care. Understanding my life's purpose is indeed a profound journey—one that requires deep introspection and self-awareness. As I reflect on what I believe my calling or ministry to be, I'm filled with a sense of gratitude for the opportunities to serve and make a positive impact.

Galatians 6:7-10 offers valuable insights into the principles of sowing and reaping. It reminds me that the seeds I sow in life will yield a harvest, whether of corruption or eternal life. It encourages me not to grow weary of doing good, for in due season, I will reap if I do not give up. This passage speaks to the importance of perseverance and resilience in living out my purpose. It inspires me to continue sowing seeds of kindness, compassion, and love, knowing that they will bear fruit in due time. Understanding my life's purpose is a journey filled with moments of clarity and revelation. It's about identifying those moments when I feel most aligned with God's will and purpose for my life. Reflecting on these moments helps me gain insight into my true calling and the impact I'm meant to make in the world. It's a journey of self-discovery and growth, one that requires patience, faith, and trust in God's guidance.

Once I have a clearer sense of my purpose, I strive to walk in it daily. I seek out opportunities to serve others and make a positive difference in their lives. Whether through volunteer work, acts of kindness, or sharing words of encouragement, I endeavor to live out my calling in tangible ways. It's about integrating my purpose into my everyday actions and interactions, infusing them with meaning and significance.

My understanding and living out my life's purpose is a journey of faith, growth, and service. It's about committing my work to the Lord, trusting in His guidance, and embracing each day with joy and enthusiasm. As I continue this journey, I'm filled with gratitude for the privilege of being a vessel for God's love and grace, and I'm inspired to continue sowing seeds of goodness wherever I go.

Lesson Learned

As I walk in my purpose, I am filled with a deep sense of joy and fulfillment. Living in alignment with God's will brings a sense of peace and contentment that transcends circumstances. It's a journey that transforms not only my own life but also the lives of those around me. I am grateful for the opportunity to make a difference, to sow seeds of love and hope in a world that often feels broken.

Reflection

Think about your life's purpose and how you can walk in it daily. What is your calling or ministry? How can you serve others and make a positive impact? Write down your thoughts on your purpose and specific steps you can take to live

Prayer

Dear Heavenly Father, We come before You with humble hearts, seeking Your guidance and blessings. Your Word in Proverbs 16:3 instructs us to "Commit your work to the Lord, and your plans will be established." Lord, we dedicate all our endeavors, plans, and actions to You. We ask for Your wisdom and direction in all that we do, trusting that You will establish our plans according to Your divine purpose.

In Galatians 6:7-10, You remind us, "Do not be deceived: God is not mocked, for whatever one sows, that will he also reap. For the one who sows to his own flesh will from the flesh reap corruption, but the one who sows to the Spirit will from the Spirit reap eternal life." Father, help us to sow seeds that are pleasing to You, seeds that reflect Your Spirit and lead to eternal life. Guard us from the temptations of the flesh and guide us to live by the Spirit.

Your Word also encourages us to "not grow weary of doing good, for in due season we will reap, if we do not give up." Lord, grant us the strength and perseverance to continue doing good, even when we face challenges and discouragement. Remind us of the eternal reward that awaits those who remain faithful and steadfast in their good works.

Finally, as Galatians 6:10 says, "So then, as we have opportunity, let us do good to everyone, and especially to those who are of the household of faith." Father, open our eyes to the opportunities around us to do good. Help us to be a blessing to others, showing kindness, compassion, and love, especially to our brothers and sisters in Christ. We commit our work, our lives, and our hearts to You, Lord. May Your will be done in and through us. We pray this in the name of Jesus Christ, our Lord and Savior. Amen.

Six

Day 5: Dating God's Way

J ames 1:5 (ESV) If any of you lacks wisdom, you should ask God, who gives generously to all without finding fault, and it will be given to you.

Proverbs 3:5-6 (ESV) Trust in the Lord with all your heart and lean not on your own understanding; in all your ways submit to him, and he will make your paths straight.

My Understanding of This Journey

Proverbs 3:5- 6 speaks to my heart, reminding me to trust in the Lord with all my heart and lean not on my own understanding. In the realm of dating and socializing, where excitement and apprehension often mingle, I find solace in surrendering my concerns and uncertainties to God. Reflecting on my current thoughts and feelings about dating, I embrace a mixture of enthusiasm, hopefulness, and perhaps a touch of nervousness. Yet, understanding these emotions allows me to approach dating with a clearer perspective rooted in trust and faith. As I ponder what I desire in a relationship and how past experiences have shaped my expectations, I trust that God will guide my steps and make my paths straight.

James 1:5 reassures me that if I lack wisdom, I need only to ask God, who gives generously to all without finding fault. Maintaining my values while navigating the realm of dating is paramount to forming genuine connections. Reflecting on the core values and principles that guide my behavior and decisions, I am reminded of the importance of honesty, respect, and mutual support. As I create a personal manifesto or list of non-negotiables, I find strength in upholding these values, knowing that they lay the foundation for healthy relationships. Recalling past experiences where I remained true to myself, I am empowered to stay grounded in my beliefs while remaining open to new possibilities. Navigating the complexities of dating and socializing can indeed feel overwhelming at times, yet seeking guidance and support from a higher power brings comfort and clarity to my journey. Reflecting on how my faith or spirituality influences my approach to dating, I find solace in prayer, reading the word, and meditating on God's word for leading and guiding.

Lesson Learned

Remembering specific instances where I felt supported or guided, I am reminded of God's presence in every aspect of my life, including my relationships. With each step, I lean on His wisdom and grace, knowing that I am never alone on this journey.

Reflection

Navigating the world of dating and socializing can be challenging. What are your thoughts and feelings about dating? How do you maintain your values while meeting new people? Reflect on your experiences and any lessons learned. Don't hesitate to ask for guidance and support from the Lord when needed.

Prayer

Dear Heavenly Father, We come before You today with hearts full of gratitude and humility. Your Word in Proverbs 3:5-6 instructs us to "Trust in the Lord with all your heart and lean not on your own understanding; in all your ways submit to him, and he will make your paths straight." Lord, we choose to trust You with all our hearts, acknowledging that our own understanding is limited. We submit all our ways to You, knowing that You will guide us and make our paths straight.

Father, we also remember the promise in James 1:5: "If any of you lacks wisdom, you should ask God, who gives generously to all without finding fault, and it will be given to you." We humbly ask for Your wisdom, Lord. We recognize our need for Your guidance and understanding in every area of our lives. Please pour out Your wisdom upon us generously, without finding fault.

Help us to lean on Your wisdom and not on our own understanding. Teach us to trust in Your plans and purposes, even when we do not fully comprehend them. Lead us in Your truth and righteousness, and let Your wisdom direct our decisions and actions.

Lord, we commit our lives, our plans, and our desires to You. We trust that You will lead us on the right path, guiding us with Your loving hand. Strengthen our faith and help us to rely on You in all circumstances. We pray this in the name of Jesus Christ, our Lord and Savior. Amen.

Seven

DAY 6: Learning to Communicate

Proverbs 18:21 (ESV) The tongue has the power of life and death, and those who love it will eat its fruit.

Proverbs 15:1 (ESV) A gentle answer turns away wrath, but a harsh word stirs up anger.

My Understanding of This Journey

Proverbs 18:21 teaches me, "The tongue has the power of life and death, and those who love it will eat its fruit." I reflect on this profound truth, understanding that communication serves as the foundation for building strong and meaningful relationships. As I contemplate my communication style, I recognize the impact it has on my interactions with others. I strive to express myself verbally and non-verbally in ways that are kind and uplifting, and I value the importance of listening and responding with empathy and love. Acknowledging my strengths, such as being empathetic, articulate, or a good listener, I also see areas for growth, like becoming more assertive or enhancing my active listening skills. Reflecting on moments where effective communication has enriched my relationships brings me joy, while I learn valuable lessons from instances where misunderstandings or conflicts arose due to poor communication.

Proverbs 15:1 reminds me that "A gentle answer turns away wrath, but a harsh word stirs up anger." Reflecting on this wisdom, I consider my approach to resolving conflicts and addressing disagreements in relationships. I seek to understand whether I tend to avoid confrontation or confront issues directly and how I can handle disagreements in a way that aligns with my values and preserves the relationship. Embracing strategies for improving conflict resolution skills, I practice active listening, express my emotions calmly and respectfully, and seek compromise or common ground. Writing about my experiences implementing these strategies, I recognize the challenges and celebrate the successes, knowing that each step brings me closer to resolving conflicts with grace and understanding.

Lesson Learned

I think about ways to enhance my communication skills and deepen my connections with others, inspired by the desire to live a godly life. I seek feedback from trusted friends or mentors, attend communication workshops or seminars, and practice mindfulness and self-awareness techniques to improve my emotional intelligence. Writing down specific goals and action steps for enhancing my communication skills, I prioritize fostering healthier relationships. By committing to effective communication, I can cultivate stronger connections and navigate relationships with greater understanding, empathy, and joy. Embracing this journey, I trust in God's guidance, knowing that my efforts will bear fruit in the form of deeper, more loving relationships.

Reflection

Effective communication is crucial for maintaining healthy relationships. How do you currently communicate with others? What are your strengths and areas for improvement? Describe your communication style and outline your strategies for improving your interactions with others.

Prayer

Dear Heavenly Father, We come before You with grateful hearts, acknowledging the wisdom You provide through Your Word. You have reminded us in Proverbs 18:21 that "The tongue has the power of life and death, and those who love it will eat its fruit." Lord, help us to be mindful of the words we speak, understanding the immense power they hold. May our words bring life, encouragement, and healing to those around us. Teach us to speak with wisdom, kindness, and love.

In Proverbs 15:1, You teach us that "A gentle answer turns away wrath, but a harsh word stirs up anger." Father, grant us the grace to respond gently in every situation. Help us to defuse anger and conflict with our words, fostering peace and understanding. Give us the strength to choose gentleness over harshness and to be instruments of Your peace in our interactions.

Lord, we ask for Your guidance in taming our tongues and using our speech to glorify You. Fill our hearts with Your love so that it overflows into our words and actions. Help us to be slow to speak, quick to listen, and always ready to offer a gentle answer.

We commit our words to You, trusting that You will guide us in using them for good. May our speech reflect Your grace and truth, bringing light and life to all we encounter.

We pray this in the name of Jesus Christ, our Lord and Savior. Amen.

Eight

DAY 7: Your Relationship with God

J ohn 1:10-13 (ESV) God created the world and gave us the right to become His children.

Romans 5:8 (ESV) God showed His love for us by sending Christ to die for us while we were still sinners.

Psalm 23:1 (ESV) God is our shepherd who guides, protects, and comforts us.

Hebrews 4:16 (ESV) We can approach God's throne of grace with confidence and receive His mercy and help.

1 Peter 5:7 (ESV) We can cast all our anxiety on God because He cares for us.

1 John 5:2-3 (ESV) We show our love for God and His children by keeping His commandments.

My Understanding of This Journey

24

In 1 John 5:2-3, it reminds me on how to show my love for God and His children by keeping His commandments. As I reflect on my journey, I realize that my relationship with God is a deeply personal and meaningful aspect of my life. Each day, I strive to connect with my faith and spirituality through practices such as prayer, meditation, scripture reading, and attending religious services. These activities anchor my day, providing me with a sense of peace and purpose.

My spirituality shapes my values, beliefs, and worldview, guiding my actions and decisions. Reflecting on the experiences and encounters that have deepened my connection with God fills my heart with joy. These moments of divine connection, whether through a powerful sermon, a quiet moment of prayer, or the beauty of nature, bring me closer to my faith and remind me of God's unwavering presence in my life.

1 Peter 5:7 invites me to cast all my anxiety on God because He cares for me. Reflecting on the challenges and obstacles I've faced on my spiritual journey, I recognize the times of doubt, questioning, and adversity. These moments, though difficult, have been pivotal in shaping my faith. Navigating these challenges required leaning heavily on God's promises and seeking comfort in His word. I am reminded of the importance of community and support in sustaining my faith during tough times. My church family, spiritual mentors, and close friends have been a source of strength and encouragement.

Writing about the moments of growth and transformation that emerged from facing adversity and seeking guidance from my faith reveals a pattern of God's grace and faithfulness. Each trial has brought me closer to Him, teaching me to trust in His plan and lean on His everlasting arms.

Romans 5:8 reveals the depth of God's love for us by sending Christ to die for us while we were still sinners. Reflecting on the moments of divine inspiration or spiritual awakening that have profoundly impacted my life, I feel a deep sense of gratitude and awe. These moments, often unexpected, provide clarity, peace, and guidance just when I need them most. Whether through a sudden realization during prayer, a verse that speaks directly to my heart, or a sense of God's presence during a quiet walk, these experiences have shaped my beliefs and influenced my decisions.

Lesson Learned

Writing about the significance of these moments, I see how they continue to inspire and guide me on my spiritual journey. Each divine encounter strengthens my faith and reminds me of God's infinite love and mercy. By documenting these reflections, I deepen my connection with God and gain insight into the ways my faith informs and enriches my life, filling it with purpose, joy, and unwavering hope.

Reflection

Reflect on your spiritual journey and relationship with God. How do you connect with your faith? What role does spirituality play in your life? Write about your experiences, challenges, and moments of divine inspiration.

Prayer

Dear Heavenly Father, We come before You with grateful hearts, acknowledging Your greatness and the profound love You have shown us. As Your Word in John 1:10-13 reminds us, you created the world and gave us the right to become Your children. We are in awe of this incredible privilege and thank You for adopting us into Your family.

Romans 5:8 reveals the depth of Your love: "But God shows his love for us in that while we were still sinners, Christ died for us." Lord, we are humbled by this ultimate sacrifice and are eternally grateful for the grace and mercy You have extended to us through Jesus Christ.

In Psalm 23:1, we are comforted by the truth that You are our Shepherd: "The Lord is my shepherd; I shall not want." You guide, protect, and comfort us, providing for all our needs. We trust in Your faithful care and leadership in our lives.

Your Word in Hebrews 4:16 encourages us to approach Your throne of grace with confidence: "Let us then with confidence draw near to the throne of grace, that we may receive mercy and find grace to help in time of need." Father, we come boldly before You, seeking Your mercy and help. We thank You for always being there for us, ready to offer Your grace and support.

1 Peter 5:7 reminds us to cast all our anxiety on You because You care for

us: "Casting all your anxieties on him because he cares for you." Lord, we surrender our worries and burdens to You, trusting in Your loving care. You know our hearts and our struggles, and we find peace in Your embrace.

In 1 John 5:2-3, we are reminded of our duty to show our love for You and Your children by keeping Your commandments: "By this we know that we love the children of God, when we love God and obey his commandments. For this is the love of God, that we keep his commandments." Help us, Lord, to live in obedience to Your Word, demonstrating our love for You and for others through our actions.

Heavenly Father, we thank You for the incredible journey You have set before us. May we walk in Your ways, guided by Your wisdom and love, always trusting in Your care and provision.

We pray this in the name of Jesus Christ, our Savior and Redeemer. Amen.

Nine

Part II: Courtship and Engaged

~⚬⚬⚬~

For those who are engaged yet still single, it can be an interesting and possibly challenging role and transition as a Christian. It is a unique season of life where you are simultaneously committed to your partner in love while navigating the final stages of single-hood. In many ways, it mirrors the transition into puberty, marked by significant physical, mental, and emotional changes. In these moments of anticipation and preparation, you learn what it means to live a God-centered life, seeking to grow deeper in knowing each other while keeping your focus firmly rooted in faith and obedience to God. This period serves as a crucial time for both partners to strengthen their individual relationships with God, ensuring a strong spiritual foundation for their future together.

Scriptural Guidance:

- *Ecclesiastes 4:9-12: "Two are better than one, because they have a good return for their labor: If either of them falls down, one can help the other up. But pity anyone who falls and has no one to help them up." This passage highlights the strength and support that comes from a committed partnership. Engaged couples can use this time to build each other up spiritually and emotionally.*

- **Proverbs 3:5-6:** *"Trust in the Lord with all your heart and lean not on your own understanding; in all your ways submit to him, and He will make your paths straight." Engaged couples are reminded to trust in God's guidance and submit their relationship to Him. This ensures that their union is rooted in God's wisdom and direction.*

Kingdom Focused Activities:

- **Premarital Counseling:** *Participate in* premarital *counseling with a focus on biblical principles to strengthen your relationship and prepare for a God-centered marriage.*
- **Joint Devotions:** *Establish a habit of praying and studying the Bible together to grow spiritually as a couple.*
- **Service Projects:** *Engage in service projects together to build teamwork and demonstrate Christ's love to others, reinforcing the importance of serving God as a united front.*

Ten

DAY 8: Courting With a Purpose

Genesis 2:24 (ESV) Therefore a man shall leave his father and his mother and hold fast to his wife, and they shall become one flesh.

1 Corinthians 13:4-6 (ESV) Love is patient and kind; love does not envy or boast; it is not arrogant or rude. It does not insist on its own way; it is not irritable or resentful; it does not rejoice at wrongdoing but rejoices with the truth.

Proverbs 18:22 (ESV) He who finds a wife finds a good thing and obtains favor from the Lord."

Mark 10:9 (ESV) Therefore what God has joined together, let no one separate.

My Understanding of This Journey

1 Corinthians 13:4-6 - Love is patient and kind; love does not envy or boast; it is not arrogant or rude. It does not insist on its own way; it is not irritable or resentful; it does not rejoice at wrongdoing but rejoices with the truth. In our relationship, I deeply appreciate how our spirituality acts

as a powerful bond that unites us. Reflecting on our shared journey, I see how our faith and the values we hold dear shape our connection during the courting process. Incorporating faith into our relationship has brought a sense of peace and harmony as we are seeking God to learn more about each other. We strive to embody the love described in 1 Corinthians 13:4-6, nurturing a relationship that is patient, kind, and grounded in truth as part of the preparation for engagement.

Each day, I am grateful for the role God plays in guiding us, and I cherish the spiritual practices that reinforce our bond. As part of the courting process, we are praying, preparing, and praising God to lead us to our purpose-filled new kingdom marriage.

In Proverbs 18:22, it states that "He who finds a wife finds a good thing and obtains favor from the Lord" and in Mark 10:9, it reads "Therefore what God has joined together, let no one separate." Our shared spiritual practices are a cornerstone of our relationship, contributing significantly to our growth and intimacy. Whether praying together, attending religious services, or engaging in heartfelt spiritual discussions, these moments of connection bring us closer. Reflecting on these practices, I see how they provide us with divine guidance and a sense of unity. Our shared faith deepens our bond, offering comfort and strength during challenging times. Each spiritual practice we engage in is a testament to our commitment to each other and to God, reinforcing the sacredness of our union.

Genesis 2:24 Therefore, a man shall leave his father and his mother and hold fast to his wife, and they shall become one flesh. Navigating our relationship with God as a couple presents both challenges and opportunities. I reflect on how we support each other's spiritual journey, encouraging growth and exploration. Through rituals, traditions, and practices, we cultivate a deeper connection with God and each other. Documenting these reflections helps us to understand our spiritual journey better and to appreciate the unique ways in which we can strengthen our bond. Our commitment to supporting each other's faith journey brings us closer, fostering a harmonious and godly relationship.

Lesson Learned

As I continue to walk this path together, I am filled with joy and gratitude for the spiritual connection we share. I am hopeful for the future, as we nurture our relationship with God and each other. My shared faith not only brings us closer but also inspires us to be better individuals and partners. Through patience, kindness, and a deep sense of empathy, I strive to build a life together that reflects the love and grace of God. By continuously reflecting on and growing in our spiritual practices, I ensure that our relationship remains strong, joyful, and harmonious.

Reflection

Reflect on your relationship with God as a couple. How do you incorporate faith into your relationship? What spiritual practices do you share, and how do they strengthen your bond? Write about the role of spirituality in your relationship journey.

Prayer

Heavenly Father, We come before You with hearts filled with gratitude for the relationships You have blessed us with. As Your Word teaches us in Genesis 2:24, You have designed us to hold fast to our loved ones, becoming one in spirit and purpose. Lord, we ask for Your guidance and strength to nurture and cherish these bonds.

Teach us, Father, to embody the love described in 1 Corinthians 13:4-6. May our love be patient and kind, free from envy and boasting. Help us to be humble, gentle, and considerate, not insisting on our own way but seeking the good of others. Remove any irritability or resentment from our hearts, and let us rejoice in the truth, celebrating each other's successes and supporting each other in times of need.

Lord, Your Word in Proverbs 18:22 reminds us that finding a spouse is a blessing and a favor from You. We thank You for the gift of companionship and ask that You help us honor and respect our spouses, seeing them as the good thing You have provided.

As we reflect on Mark 10:9, we pray that You protect the sanctity of our relationships. What You have joined together, let no one separate. Bind us together with cords of love that cannot be broken and help us to grow closer to You and each other every day.

May our relationships reflect Your love and grace, drawing others to You through the love we share. We ask all these things in the name of Your Son, Jesus Christ. Amen.

Eleven

Day 9: Growing Closer to God in a Courtship

1 Thessalonians 5:11 (ESV) Therefore encourage one another and build one another up, just as you are doing.

John 13:34 (ESV) A new commandment I give to you, that you love one another: just as I have loved you, you also are to love one another.

Ephesians 4:2 (ESV) With all humility and gentleness, with patience, bearing with one another in love. Make every effort to keep the unity of the Spirit through the bond of peace.

Ecclesiastes 4:10 (ESV) For if they fall, one will lift his fellow. But woe to him who is alone when he falls and has not another to lift him up!

Proverbs 13:20 (NIV) Whoever walks with the wise becomes wise, but the companion of fools will suffer harm.

My Understanding of This Journey

In Proverbs 13:20, it reads that "Whoever walks with the wise becomes wise, but the companion of fools will suffer harm." Entering an engagement marks a significant milestone in my relationship journey. As I take this moment to reflect, I am filled with gratitude and joy for the path we've walked together. From our initial dates filled with excitement and discovery to the profound decision to commit to a future together, every step has been a blessing. I cherish the values, goals, and shared experiences that have shaped our relationship into something beautiful and enduring. Thinking about the qualities that drew us to each other and continue to strengthen our bond fills me with appreciation. Your kindness, wisdom, and unwavering support are just a few of the many reasons I love you. Together, we have cultivated a partnership rooted in love, respect, and mutual growth.

In Ecclesiastes 4:10, it states "For if they fall, one will lift his fellow. But woe to him who is alone when he falls and has not another to lift him up! Reflecting on the dynamics of our relationship, I see how we support and uplift each other in so many ways." We are a team, always ready to lend a hand, offer a comforting word, or share in each other's joys and sorrows. Communication, trust, and mutual respect form the strong foundation of our relationship. I appreciate how we actively work to understand and meet each other's needs, and I am grateful for the patience and grace we extend to one another. As we look to the future, I am filled with hope and excitement. Our shared dreams and aspirations will guide us as we build a life together grounded in love and faith.

Ephesians 4:2 - With all humility and gentleness, with patience, bearing with one another in love. Make every effort to keep the unity of the Spirit through the bond of peace.

Lesson Learned

Considering how our relationship reflects our individual identities and values, I see a beautiful balance between independence and partnership. We celebrate each other's unique strengths and support one another through challenges and joys. Our relationship is enriched by the rituals, traditions, and shared experiences that bring us closer. Whether it's a weekly date night, a heartfelt conversation, or simply enjoying each other's company, these moments define our bond and deepen our connection. By documenting these reflections, I reaffirm my commitment to you and our journey together. With God's guidance, our love will continue to grow, rooted in humility, gentleness, and patience, creating a peaceful and joyful future together.

Reflection

As you transition from being single to being engaged, reflect on what your relationship looks like now. How has it evolved since you were single? What are the dynamics and aspects that define your relationship? Write about the strengths, challenges, and aspirations you have as a couple.

Prayer

Dear Heavenly Father, We come before You with thankful hearts, grateful for the guidance and wisdom found in Your Word. We are reminded in 1 Thessalonians 5:11 to "encourage one another and build one another up, just as you are doing." Lord, help us to be sources of encouragement and support to those around us, building each other up in faith and love.

In John 13:34, Jesus gave us a new commandment: "A new commandment I give to you, that you love one another: just as I have loved you, you also are to love one another." Father, fill our hearts with Your love so that we may love others as Jesus has loved us. Let our actions reflect the selfless, unconditional love that You have shown us.

Ephesians 4:2-3 reminds us to live "with all humility and gentleness, with patience, bearing with one another in love. Make every effort to keep the unity of the Spirit through the bond of peace." Lord, grant us the humility, gentleness, and patience to bear with one another in love. Help us to strive for unity and peace in all our relationships, guided by Your Spirit.

In Ecclesiastes 4:10, we learn the importance of companionship: "For if they fall, one will lift up his fellow. But woe to him who is alone when he falls and has not another to lift him up!" Father, we thank You for the gift of community and friendship. Help us to be there for one another, lifting each other up in times of need and sharing in each other's joys and sorrows.

Proverbs 13:20 teaches us that "Whoever walks with the wise becomes wise, but the companion of fools will suffer harm." Lord, give us the wisdom to choose our companions wisely. Surround us with those who will guide us in Your ways and help us to grow in wisdom and righteousness.

Heavenly Father, we ask for Your strength and guidance as we seek to live out these principles in our daily lives. May we be instruments of Your love, peace, and encouragement, always seeking to uplift and support those around us. We pray this in the name of Jesus Christ, our Lord and Savior. Amen.

Twelve

DAY 10: Praying Together

Matthew 6:6 (NIV) But when you pray, go into your room and shut the door and pray to your Father who is in secret. And your Father who sees in secret will reward you.

James 5:16 (ESV) Therefore, confess your sins to one another and pray for one another, that you may be healed.

1 Thessalonians 5:16-18 (ESV) Rejoice evermore. Pray without ceasing. In everything give thanks: for this is the will of God in Christ Jesus concerning you.

My Understanding of This Journey

In 1 Thessalonians 5:16-18 it reads "Rejoice evermore. Pray without ceasing. In everything give thanks: for this is the will of God in Christ Jesus concerning you". Prayer is such a powerful tool for deepening our connection as a couple and inviting divine guidance and blessings into our relationship. When we pray together, I feel an immense sense of joy and gratitude, knowing we are placing our trust in God. Reflecting on these moments, I am reminded of the spiritual intimacy we share, how our hearts align, and how our bond strengthens. I treasure the times we seek God's will for our lives, rejoicing together in the good times and supporting each other through challenges. These moments of prayer are sacred, nurturing our love and bringing us closer to each other and to God.

In James 5:16, it states "Therefore, confess your sins to one another and pray for one another, that you may be healed". Our rituals and practices of praying together have become a cornerstone of our relationship. Whether we have regular prayer times or spontaneously lift each other up in prayer, these acts of faith bring us comfort and healing. I cherish the times we support each other spiritually, confessing our struggles and seeking God's guidance. Through prayer, we find strength and encouragement, knowing we are not alone in our journey. My heart is filled with hope and love as I think about our shared commitment to each other's spiritual growth and well-being, always seeking God's blessings for our future. Matthew 6:6 – But when you pray, go into your room and shut the door and pray to your Father who is in secret. And your father who sees in secret will reward you.

Lesson Learned

Cultivating spiritual intimacy in our relationship presents both challenges and opportunities. Prayer helps us navigate disagreements, seek forgiveness, and grow closer to each other and to God. Reflecting on our journey, I see how our private moments of prayer strengthen our public life together. We can always deepen our practice of praying together, ensuring that our relationship remains grounded in faith and love. Documenting these reflections, I feel inspired to nurture the spiritual foundation of our relationship, drawing strength and joy from our shared faith. Through God's grace, we continue to grow in love and unity, cherishing each moment and looking forward to the blessings ahead.

Reflection

Reflect on the significance of praying together and praying for each other in your relationship. How does prayer strengthen your bond as a couple? What intentions and blessings do you seek for each other? Write about the importance of spiritual intimacy in your relationship journey.

Prayer

Dear Heavenly Father, We come before You in reverence and humility, seeking Your presence and guidance in our lives. As You have instructed us in Matthew 6:6, we find solace in retreating to a quiet place, shutting the door, and praying to You in secret. We are grateful for the assurance that You, who sees what is done in secret, will reward us openly. Help us to cultivate a personal and intimate relationship with You through these private moments of prayer.

Lord, Your Word in James 5:16 encourages us to confess our sins to one another and pray for each other so that we may be healed. We ask for the courage to be vulnerable and honest with one another, sharing our struggles and lifting each other up in prayer. Let Your healing power flow through our confessions and prayers, bringing restoration and wholeness to our lives and relationships.

In 1 Thessalonians 5:16-18, You call us to rejoice always, pray continually, and give thanks in all circumstances, for this is Your will for us in Christ Jesus. Fill our hearts with joy and gratitude, even during challenges and uncertainties. Teach us to pray without ceasing, making our communication with You a constant and natural part of our daily lives.

We thank You, Lord, for the privilege of talking to You, knowing that You hear us and care deeply for us. May our prayers be filled with faith, hope, and love, drawing us closer to You and aligning our hearts with Your will.

In the precious name of Jesus, we pray. Amen.

Thirteen

Day 11: During Courtship

∾⟨⟨∾⟩⟩∾

1 Thessalonians 5:16-18 (NIV) Rejoice always, pray continually, give thanks in all circumstances; for this is God's will for you in Christ Jesus.

My Understanding of This Journey

Navigating social events requires a delicate balance between learning about yourselves and your person. It takes self-awareness to stay true to oneself while engaging with others. As I write this, I reflect on past experiences attending holidays, functions, and events. I consider the moments where I felt most comfortable and authentic, as well as times when I struggled to maintain my sense of self amidst distractions and the overwhelming feeling of being single—not because I'm unhappy, but because of the noise from others. In my journal, I am clear that while I enjoy the holidays, I often pray for them to pass quickly due to the pressure and questions about my happiness. My best advice to myself and others is to enjoy life and stay connected to Jesus. This is the perfect time to practice self-care and engage in activities that bring joy.

I think about the aspects of social events that bring me joy and fulfillment. Is it connecting with friends and family, engaging in meaningful conversations, or participating in activities that I enjoy? I reflect on the moments where I felt most connected and engaged with others, cherishing those experiences. Considering how I can replicate these moments in future social settings enhances my overall enjoyment and satisfaction. It's about finding those joyful connections and holding onto them, even amid busy gatherings.

Anticipating upcoming holidays, functions, and events with a positive mindset helps me plan. I set intentions for how I want to show up authentically and engage with others in ways that align with my values and goals. I consider strategies for managing stress or anxiety, such as practicing mindfulness techniques, setting boundaries, or taking breaks when needed. By writing down specific goals and action steps for navigating upcoming social events, I approach these gatherings with confidence and grace. This intentional approach allows me to foster meaningful connections and create lasting memories, making each event a joyous occasion.

Lesson Learned

By reflecting on past experiences and planning for future ones, I can navigate social events with joy and grace. Staying connected to Jesus, practicing self-care, and being intentional about my interactions help me stay true to myself. This journey of self-awareness and faith guides me through each holiday and event, turning them into opportunities for genuine connection and happiness.

Reflection

Social events can be both enjoyable and overwhelming. How do you navigate holidays, functions, and events? What strategies help you stay true to yourself in these settings? Reflect on past experiences and plan for upcoming events with a positive mindset.

Prayer

Heavenly Father, We come before You with hearts full of gratitude, seeking Your presence and guidance. Your Word in 1 Thessalonians 5:16-18 instructs us to rejoice always, pray continually, and give thanks in all circumstances, for this is Your will for us in Christ Jesus. We ask that You help us to live out these commands in our daily lives.

Lord, fill our hearts with joy that surpasses all understanding, enabling us to rejoice always, regardless of our circumstances. Teach us to find joy in Your presence, Your promises, and the blessings You have bestowed upon us.

Help us, Father, to cultivate a spirit of continual prayer. May our hearts be attuned to You throughout each day, lifting our thoughts, concerns, and praises to You without ceasing. Let our lives be a testament to our dependence on You, seeking Your guidance and strength in every situation.

We also ask for a heart of gratitude, Lord. Remind us to give thanks in all circumstances, recognizing Your hand at work in every aspect of our lives. Help us to see Your goodness even in challenging times and to trust that You are working all things for our good and Your glory.

Thank You, Father, for the gift of Your Son, Jesus Christ, through whom we have the assurance of Your love and the hope of eternal life. May our lives reflect Your will as we rejoice, pray, and give thanks.

In Jesus' name, we pray. Amen.

Fourteen

Day 12: Relationship with God

1 John 2:6 (NKJV) He who says he abides in Him ought himself also to walk just as He walked.

My Understanding of This Journey

The best way for me to describe this journey and My Understanding of this Journey is to first talk about my misunderstanding of what I thought it meant to have a relationship with Christ. When I was much younger, I didn't know what it meant to have a relationship with God. I thought that my simple belief that God exists was enough. I felt that I was living just fine because I believed that God exists and I attended church sometimes with family members. Fast forward to when I committed my life to Jesus Christ years later. It was at that time that I learned what a relationship with Jesus Christ was all about, **and I'M STILL LEARNING**! Having a relationship with Jesus Christ includes me surrendering myself (my problems, thoughts, decisions, and plans) to God. Having a relationship with God isn't something that takes a break or day off; it's a consistent act.

In my daily surrender, I give everything to God, or at least I make the effort to give everything to God. I give my morning to God. I give my day to God. I give my evening to God. I give my choices to God. I ask God for help.

I depend on God's answer. I expect God's answer! I look to God to help me decide whether I should take this job? Should I get into a new business opportunity? I give God even the smallest decisions, such as, "What verse would you like me to study in the Bible today, Lord?"

Lesson Learned

Having a relationship with God means that I am not living without inviting God into my daily life so that I can depend on Him by asking and seeking the Lord daily. It simply means I am not living this life alone. I choose to live this life that I live because my life is not my own. This life that I live belongs to Jesus Christ, as He is the one who gave me life.

Reflection

Walking as Jesus walked requires us to love our neighbors, forgive freely, and serve selflessly. It means aligning our actions, words, and thoughts with His. This alignment comes from a deep relationship with Him, nurtured through prayer, Scripture, and community. Let this verse remind us daily to live in a way that honors Jesus, reflecting His light and love to the world.

Prayer

Dear Lord, I thank You for giving me this life and for blessing me abundantly. I am grateful for Your constant presence, never leaving me alone. Thank You for always answering when I seek Your help and for the sacrifice of Your Son, Jesus Christ, who died on the cross for my sins, granting me a life full of freedom and joy.

Lord, as Your Word in 1 John 2:6 reminds us, "He who says he abides in Him ought himself also to walk just as He walked." I pray that my life reflects Your love and grace, striving to walk as Jesus did in love, humility, and obedience. Help me to honor You in all that I do.

I pray, Father, for someone reading this prayer, that they may realize Your immense love for them. You have given them life, and I pray they will surrender themselves to You daily, embracing the joy and freedom found in a relationship with You.

In Jesus Christ's name, I pray. Amen.

Fifteen

Part III: Dating with Children

Dating with children introduces a unique set of challenges and considerations that require careful navigation. Balancing the responsibilities of parenthood with the desire to build a new romantic relationship can be complex. It is essential to approach this period with sensitivity, wisdom, and a strong foundation in faith to ensure the well-being of both the children and the relationship. An integral part of this process is having a network of godly social support to provide practical help, emotional encouragement, and spiritual guidance. This support system plays a crucial role in helping parents navigate the complexities of dating with children while maintaining a strong faith and family foundation.

Scriptural Guidance:

Proverbs 22:6: *"Start children off on the way they should go, and even when they are old, they will not turn from it. This verse emphasizes the importance of providing a stable and loving environment for children. When dating with children, it is crucial to prioritize their needs and ensure they feel secure and loved. Guiding children with love and consistency helps them develop a strong moral foundation and a sense of security, which is vital when introducing changes such as a new* *partner.*

Colossians 3:21: *"Fathers, do not embitter your children, or they will become discouraged."This passage reminds parents to be mindful of their children's emotional well-being. Introducing a new partner should be done with care and consideration to avoid causing confusion or distress. Taking the time to listen to your children's feelings and concerns is essential in fostering a supportive and understanding family environment during this transition.*

Psalm 127:3: *"Children are a heritage from the Lord, offspring a reward from him."Viewing children as a blessing helps in making decisions that honor their importance in your life. Any new relationship should respect and nurture this precious heritage. Recognizing the value and gift of children encourages parents to make thoughtful choices that protect and enhance their children's lives.*

Kingdom Focused Activities:

- **Open Communication:** *Be honest with your children about your dating intentions. Age-appropriate conversations can help them understand and feel included in this new chapter of your life. Transparency fosters trust and helps alleviate any fears or uncertainties your children might have.*
- **Gradual Introduction:** *Introduce your new partner gradually. Ensure your children have time to adjust and feel comfortable with the changes in their family dynamics. Gradual integration allows for natural relationship development and reduces potential anxiety or resistance from the children.*
- **Prioritize Quality Time:** *Continue to spend quality time with your children. Reassure them that your love and commitment to them remain unchanged. Maintaining regular, special moments with your children reinforces their sense of security and helps them feel valued and prioritized.*
- **Seek God's Guidance:** *Pray for wisdom and discernment in your relationship. Seek God's guidance in making decisions that are in the best interest of your children and your future. Trusting in God's plan provides clarity and peace, ensuring that your actions align with His will.*

- **Support System**: *Lean on a support system of family, friends, and church community. They can provide valuable advice, support, and encouragement as you navigate dating with children. Engaging with a godly support system offers multiple benefits, including practical help, emotional support, and spiritual guidance.*

Importance of Godly Social Support:

Having a network of godly social support is crucial when dating with children. This network can provide:

- **Practical Help**: *Trusted friends and family members can assist with childcare, offering you time to nurture your new relationship while ensuring your children are well-cared for.*
- **Emotional Support**: *Dating as a single parent can be emotionally taxing. A godly support system offers a safe space to share your feelings, seek advice, and receive encouragement.*
- **Spiritual Guidance**: *Fellow believers can pray with you and for you, offering spiritual wisdom and insights grounded in biblical principles. Their guidance can help you stay rooted in faith, making decisions that honor God and benefit your family.*
- **Accountability**: *A supportive community can help you stay accountable in maintaining your values and commitments. They can provide gentle reminders to keep your priorities in line with your faith and family responsibilities.*
- **Encouragement**: *Positive reinforcement from a godly community can boost your confidence and help you stay motivated in your journey. Their encouragement can remind you of God's promises and the importance of perseverance.*

By incorporating these practices and seeking godly social support, you can create a balanced and loving environment that supports both your children's needs and your personal growth in a new relationship. A strong network of believers helps ensure that your decisions are aligned with God's will, fostering a healthy and

God-centered family dynamic.

Kingdom Focused Activities:

- **Family Devotions:** *Engage in regular family devotions, including your children in prayer and Bible study. This not only strengthens your faith but also sets a godly example for your children.*
- **Church Involvement:** *Participate in church activities and services together as a family. Being active in a faith community provides spiritual nourishment and a sense of belonging for both you and your children.*
- **Service Projects:** *Volunteer for service projects as a family. Serving others together can build unity and demonstrate Christ's love, teaching children the importance of compassion and generosity.*
- **Faith-Based Counseling:** *Seek faith-based counseling to address any family dynamics and relationship concerns. Counseling grounded in biblical principles can provide valuable insights and strategies for maintaining a healthy family environment.*
- **Christian Fellowship:** *Engage in fellowship with other Christian families. Sharing experiences and building friendships with other believers can provide support, encouragement, and a strong sense of community.*

Sixteen

DAY 13: Single With Children

J oshua 1:9 (NKJV) Have I not commanded you? Be strong and of good courage; do not be afraid, nor be dismayed, for the Lord your God is with you wherever you go.

Isaiah 41:10 (NKJV) Fear not, for I am with you; Be not dismayed, for I am your God. I will strengthen you, yes, I will help you, I will uphold you with My righteous right hand.

My Understanding of This Journey

The moment I realized that I was going to become a single parent, I believed that it wouldn't be difficult. I believed that it would be something that not only could I do alone, but I also believed that I would be just fine alone parenting a child and not asking for help. It didn't take long for me to discover that my pride was useless because pride never bought groceries, comforted my babies when they were sick, or paid the bills. It wasn't until I discovered I was expecting twins when everything shifted in one blink of an eye. I had spent my younger life very much curious about what God wanted me to do. I wondered who God would bring into my life and why.

Growing up in a large family, children were always around. I was always surrounded by so many different personalities and characters who always seemed so carefree! I'd spend time with aunts, uncles, cousins thinking about how they made parenting look so effortless! I was wrong. When I became a mother, I realized that parenting was very challenging yet very rewarding; exhausting at times yet filled with energetic joy. Nothing is ever as easy as it looks.

Nothing. I wasn't alone, I had God's love and grace. God gave me everything my pride could never deliver. I'm grateful to God for every moment that humbled me to receive His blessings and guidance. My journey was nothing short of a huge miracle.

Lesson Learned

God can step into any situation and create an outcome that benefits you but more importantly, will glorify Him. When you face challenges as a parent, give those challenges to God and watch what God does.

Reflection

God can step into any situation and create outcomes that benefit us and glorify Him. As parents, we face many challenges, but we are not alone. When we surrender our struggles to God, we invite His wisdom and strength into our lives. Trusting Him with our parenting challenges allows us to see His faithfulness and experience His peace. Let us lean on God, knowing He will guide us and bring glory to His name.

Prayer

Dear Lord, I pray that you help the single-parents that are raising their children, leading and managing their homes, navigating the complexities of parenthood, through all the ups and downs of parenthood.

I pray Father, that you remind every single parent that you're right next to them. Remind them that your Holy Spirit is available to help them in every situation. Remind them that Jesus loves them so very much and wants the absolute best for them and gave his life as a sacrifice, so that they can receive peace, wisdom, confidence and patience from you. Remind them they can have the gift of forgiveness and that they will always have an inexhaustible source they can count on.

Thank you Lord for giving your strength, for giving your courage, for lifting up every parent when they need you and even when they don't need you, I pray Lord that you will inspire every single-parent to teach their children about the importance of who you are and who your son Jesus Christ was, is, and will always be.

Lord, deliver more blessings to them and their children in the name of Jesus. I say this prayer. Amen.

Seventeen

DAY 14: Creating a Support System

P roverbs 27:17 (ESV) As iron sharpens iron, so a man sharpens the countenance of his friend.

My Understanding of This Journey

My understanding of what a support system should look like has definitely been a journey. I needed people who would be there for me when I needed it and to help me when I asked. My family was the closest to me geographically but as a young adult and at times it felt as though they were a bit too close to me. I focused more on being independent and whenever I chose to "take a break" from my family circles it was during which I felt misunderstood. As I grew older and started my journey walking with Jesus Christ, I experienced the importance of having a healthy community of believers that I can fellowship with, learn from and even welcome selected women of God to hold me accountable.

Outside of my biological family, it was the first time I realized the value of having a spiritual support system. When I feel misunderstood, I now know that God understands me perfectly and my community reminds me that people may not always understand one another but we can take confidence in having meaningful conversations with one another that are life-giving, supportive and most importantly, encouraged by God.

Lesson Learned

I learned that creating a support system and having a strong group of men and women of God in your corner is paramount to living a healthy Christian lifestyle….a lifestyle that enhances God's Kingdom.

Reflection

Proverbs 27:17 says, "As iron sharpens iron, so a man sharpens the countenance of his friend." This verse emphasizes the importance of friendships in our growth. True friends challenge, support, and refine us, helping us become better. Cherish and invest in your friendships. They are essential for personal and spiritual growth, reflecting God's love and wisdom.

Prayer

Father in the name of Jesus, Show Your children the importance of having a strong community of people that love and depend on You, Lord. As Your Word says in Proverbs 27:17, "As iron sharpens iron, so a man sharpens the countenance of his friend."

I pray that You will change, build, and create a healthy support system for me and all Your children who are single parents. May we find strength and encouragement in each other, growing together in faith and love.

I pray this in Jesus Christ's name. Amen.

Eighteen

Day 15: Know Who You Are

R omans 8:37 (NKJV): Yet in all these things we are more than conquerors through Him who loved us.

My Understanding of This Journey

I must admit I didn't always understand what it meant to answer the question: "Who are you?" I was certain that I was a lot of things. I am a daughter. I am a parent. I am a sister. I am a cousin, etc. But, in all those titles I realized that's exactly what they are-titles. Those titles don't tell anybody who I am, and I wasn't able to communicate who I was because I didn't know who I was. So now that I know who I am, I know exactly who my Creator is and most importantly I know who I belong to I understand that it is critical that everyone knows who they are. When we know who we are we must also learn how God sees us and God sees us as his children.

God paid a great price for us. God wants us to succeed in this life. God has given us the ability to do things on our own; however, God wants us to connect with him and have a relationship with him so that we learn that we cannot have an identity without God. Understand this: You are part of a great Kingdom; God's Kingdom and you must know exactly who you are in Jesus Christ. Jesus Christ is the most important thing you need to know about your identity because He died for you to have the life you have now.

Lesson Learned

I learned that the world will call you many things. the world will give you many names. It's important that I answer to my name. Who am I? Answer: I am God's beloved child. I am the chosen, blood bought child of Jesus Christ! I am blessed. I am chosen. I am victorious. I can do everything through Jesus Christ. I am so much more than the world could ever name me.

Reflection

I once struggled to answer the question, "Who are you?" I identified with titles like daughter, parent, and sister, but these didn't define who I truly was. Understanding my Creator and my belonging to Him revealed my identity. It's essential to know who we are and how God sees us—as His beloved children. God wants us to succeed and have a relationship with Him. Without God, our identity is incomplete. Remember, you are part of God's Kingdom. Your identity in Jesus Christ is crucial because He died to give your life. Embrace who you are in Christ.

Prayer

Dear Lord Jesus, I pray that You help me to see myself the way that You see me. Help me to communicate clearly who I am in You, Lord. I pray that I am always aware of Your love for me and recognize that nothing can separate me from it. Thank You for calling me forgiven when I ask for forgiveness and for always loving me as Your child. Help me to always honor You in all that I do.

Thank You for making me more than a conqueror through Your love, as Your Word says in Romans 8:37, "Yet in all these things we are more than conquerors through Him who loved us."

I say this prayer in Jesus' name. Amen.

Nineteen

DAY 16: Live Your Life Fully

J ohn 14:21 (NKJV) He who has My commandments and keeps them, it is he who loves Me. And he who loves Me will be loved by My Father, and I will love him and manifest Myself to him.

Psalms 16:11 (NKJV) You will show me the path of life; In Your presence is fullness of joy; At Your right hand are pleasures forevermore.

My Understanding of This Journey

Without God, the world can be cold and scary sometimes. When we live our lives without acknowledging God and His commandments, we will always be restricted from realizing God's goodness. We need God to live a life that pleases Him, a life full of blessings and joy. Happiness is temporary. Joy in the Lord is everlasting. When we trust God, we're able to discover how fulfilling it is to live life under God's care instead of living under the care of the world.

Lesson Learned

God has nothing but good intentions for you. God's intentions for you are better than you could ever want or imagine for yourself. When we live fully, we cannot do this until we surrender our lives to God and try to obey God's commands. To live your life fully is to live in God's fullness of joy.

Reflection

Without God, the world can be cold and scary at times. When we live our lives without acknowledging God and His commandments, we restrict ourselves from realizing His goodness. We need God to live a life that pleases Him, a life full of blessings and joy. Happiness is temporary, but joy in the Lord is everlasting. When we trust God, we discover how fulfilling it is to live under His care instead of the care of the world. Embracing God's guidance brings us true peace and contentment that the world cannot offer.

Prayer

Dear Heavenly Father, I come before You with a heart open to Your guidance and wisdom. Your Word in John 14:21 tells us, "He who has My commandments and keeps them, it is he who loves Me. And he who loves Me will be loved by My Father, and I will love him and manifest Myself to him." Lord, I desire to be someone who keeps Your commandments and shows my love for You through obedience. Please help me to know and understand Your commandments for my life.

Father, Your presence is where I find true joy, as Psalm 16:11 states, "You will show me the path of life; In Your presence is fullness of joy; At Your right hand are pleasures forevermore." I seek the fullness of joy that comes from being in Your presence. Guide me on the path of life that You have set before me, and help me to stay close to You, experiencing the pleasures of Your right hand.

Lord, I pray that You will teach me and show me that my life will never be lived fully without You. Guide me to find what Your commands are for my life so that I may obey You, Lord. I ask for the revelation of Your will and purpose for me. Show me how You would like me to live fully according to Your plan, Your will, and Your purpose. Help me to surrender my desires and plans to You, trusting that Your ways are higher and better than mine. Fill me with the wisdom and strength to follow Your commands and live a life that brings glory to Your name.

Thank You for Your love and for the promise that You will manifest Yourself to those who love and obey You. I long to experience more of Your presence in my life. Guide me, teach me, and fill me with Your Spirit.

In Jesus Christ's name, I pray. Amen.

Twenty

Day 17: Walking in Your Purpose

1 Peter 4:10 (NKJV) As each one has received a gift, minister it to one another, as good stewards of the manifold grace of God.

My Understanding of This Journey

Serving in ministry is a decision that shouldn't be taken lightly. Serving in God's Kingdom can be rewarding but it comes with great responsibility. The same applies to starting a ministry. I had to receive rigorous training when I began serving. I understand how important it is to learn what your spiritual gifts are. We have unique, God given gifts that were purposely gifted to us to use in God's Kingdom. Without knowing your gifts, the further you are from learning about your God given purpose. It's crucial to your spiritual growth to invest time in learning how you can walk effectively in your purpose so that you can contribute your best to a ministry.

Lesson Learned

When you consider serving in a ministry, pray and seek the Lord FIRST! If you decide to start a ministry, make sure you talk with a trusted pastor or biblical counselor first so that you can receive help, prayer, resources, and most importantly guidance. Once you begin serving, make sure that you align your gifts and talents with how you give your time and employ accountability partners to help you as you walk in your purpose.

Reflection

Serving in ministry is a decision that shouldn't be taken lightly. While it can be incredibly rewarding, it also comes with great responsibility. The same applies to starting a ministry. When I began serving, I underwent rigorous training, which helped me understand the importance of learning about my spiritual gifts. Each of us has unique, God-given gifts, intentionally bestowed upon us to use in God's Kingdom. Without knowing these gifts, we distance ourselves from discovering our God-given purpose. It's crucial for our spiritual growth to invest time in learning how to walk effectively in our purpose. By doing so, we can contribute our best to a ministry and truly serve God's Kingdom.

Prayer

Dear Lord, I come before You, seeking Your help to discover the gifts You bestowed upon me when You created me. Your Word in 1 Peter 4:10 reminds us, "As each one has received a gift, minister it to one another, as good stewards of the manifold grace of God." I pray that You help me learn how to use my gifts and talents to serve You and Your kingdom.

Lord, I ask that I grow into my gifts and receive guidance from Your Holy Spirit. Lead me to a strong community that will support and sharpen me, so that I may become equipped to contribute my best to Your kingdom. Grant me Your wisdom and courage, and increase my ability to learn more every day, becoming a better servant for You.

I say this prayer in Jesus Christ's name. Amen.

Twenty-One

DAY 18: Dating with a Child

James 1:27 (NKJV) Pure and undefiled religion before God and the Father is this: to visit orphans and widows in their trouble, and to keep oneself unspotted from the world.

My Understanding of This Journey

Before taking the leap into dating, it's best to spend time working on becoming the best you can be in preparation. Preparing yourself takes time. You need to be healthy. If you haven't started a health journey, now is the time! Your spiritual, physical, emotional, and psychological well-being must be examined and addressed before embarking on the dating journey. Seek guidance to create your health journey. This can be a difficult journey based on your outlook and where you are in your walk with the Lord, but you can't afford to skip this step.

There are many choices you must consider when dating as a single parent. Choosing to make decisions that won't negatively impact you or your children is important and feasible! Choosing to honor God is most important. You must also choose to honor yourself and your children. All these decisions point to one question: Are you going to seek and obey God in the dating process? Prayer is key and keeping trusted accountability partners essential to successful and healthy dating. God is your anchor, trust God and rely on the Holy Spirit. God wants to take care of you so allow God into your decision-making.

Lesson Learned

I learned from experience how important it is to determine your goals when you consider dating. What do you want your outcome to look like? Are you seeking a husband or long-term relationship? Create and maintain healthy boundaries for yourself and your children. Always enlist the help of your pastor and biblical counselor. Most importantly, spend time with God, develop new habits that support your time with God and your health journey.

Reflection

Through experience, I learned the importance of determining your goals when considering dating. Ask yourself, what do you want your outcome to look like? Are you seeking a husband or a long-term relationship? Establish and maintain healthy boundaries for yourself and your children. Always seek guidance from your pastor and a biblical counselor. Most importantly, spend time with God, develop new habits that support your spiritual growth, and prioritize your health journey. These steps are crucial for creating a meaningful and fulfilling relationship that aligns with your values and goals.

Prayer

Father in the name of Jesus, I pray for Your help and guidance. Your Word in James 1:27 teaches us that pure and undefiled religion before You is to visit orphans and widows in their trouble and to keep oneself unspotted from the world. Lord, help me to live a life that reflects this pure and undefiled religion. Guide me as I prepare myself for the person I hope to meet and spend the rest of my life with as a spouse and partner. I pray that my future spouse will be working on themselves to become better for You. Grant me direction and wisdom to understand everything I have to offer and to heal in areas that are unhealthy.

I trust You, Lord, to provide me with everything I need as I learn and discover how to become a better mate for my future spouse and partner. Help me to live a life that honors You and reflects Your love and care for others.

In the name of Jesus Christ, I pray. Amen.

Twenty-Two

DAY 19: Your Relationship with God

Psalms 77:12 (NKJV) I will also meditate on all Your work, and talk of Your deeds

Joshua 1:8 (NKJV) I will meditate on Your precepts and contemplate Your ways.

Psalms 119:15 (NKJV) This Book of the Law shall not depart from your mouth, but you shall meditate in it day and night, that you may observe to do according to all that is written in it. For then you will make your way prosperous, and then you will have good success."

Psalms 119:99 (NKJV) I have more understanding than all my teachers, for Your testimonies are my meditation

My Understanding of This Journey

Having a relationship with God is a life-long journey. I realized that I cannot go through life without having a relationship with Jesus Christ. I recall the days when I was living without communicating with God daily. I didn't always depend on God. I realized that God is more faithful and trustworthy than I could ever be. It was only through my failures without God, that I understood how God used those failures to lead towards pursuing a relationship with God. I am still pursuing my relationship and growing in my relationship with Jesus Christ every day. My life has become extremely blessed, only because of my relationship with Jesus Christ.

Lesson Learned

We are called to have a relationship with God. The most important relationship that we can have as believers in Christ is the relationship that we have with God. We can take our own advice; we can follow our own ways and we can even make up our own plans. But, without the guidance of God and without the relationship and closeness that is needed to have a successful and abundant life as the Bible says, we must make every effort to have a dedicated and committed relationship with God.

Reflection

We are called to have a relationship with God. The most important relationship we can have as believers in Christ is with Him. We can take our own advice, follow our own ways, and make our own plans. However, without God's guidance and the relationship and closeness needed for a successful and abundant life, we fall short of what He desires for us. The Bible emphasizes the need for a dedicated and committed relationship with God. Let us make every effort to nurture this relationship, seeking His presence and guidance in all we do.

Prayer

Father, in the name of Jesus, I pray that You help me to grow and move closer to You. I thank You for Your love, grace, and mercy. Thank You, Lord, for creating me and for always being with me. I need Your help, Lord. Please help me. As Your Word in Psalms 77:12 says, "I will also meditate on all Your work, and talk of Your deeds." Help me to meditate on Your works and speak of Your deeds daily.

Joshua 1:8 reminds me, "This Book of the Law shall not depart from your mouth, but you shall meditate in it day and night, that you may observe to do according to all that is written in it. For then you will make your way prosperous, and then you will have good success." Guide me to spend time daily in Your Word and to learn Your ways so that I may observe to do according to all that is written in it. Psalms 119:15 says, "I will meditate on Your precepts and contemplate Your ways." Help me to understand Your precepts and contemplate Your ways, seeking deeper knowledge and wisdom from You.

And as Psalms 119:99 declares, "I have more understanding than all my teachers, For Your testimonies are my meditation." Let Your testimonies be my meditation, increasing my understanding and drawing me closer to You. Thank You, Lord, for always being with me and never leaving my side.
I pray this in Jesus Christ's name. Amen.

Twenty-Three

Day 20: Holidays and Dating

~⊛~

1 Timothy 6:6-8 (NKJV) Now godliness with contentment is great gain. For we brought nothing into this world, and it is certain we can carry nothing out. And having food and clothing, with these we shall be content.

My Understanding of This Journey

Holidays are a time to spend with family, but they can also be a period where many feel discouraged due to financial and societal pressures. These pressures can make the holiday season challenging and stressful. However, with the right encouragement, mindset, and tools, these times and the accompanying gatherings and events can be managed successfully. By focusing on meaningful connections, wise spending, and creating traditions that align with one's values, individuals can navigate the holiday season with greater ease and joy.

Lesson Learned

Never subscribe to any pressure that goes against the will of God. Do not accept financial pressure to buy physical gifts. God's best gifts are the gifts that are eternal! Do not fall into the trap of comparing yourself to others. Focus on what it means to God when spending time with family and loved ones during the holidays. Create memories and beware of any gatherings that are more transactional than relational. Create and manage your boundaries wisely and ask God to help.

Reflection

Holidays are a time to spend with family, but they can also bring financial and societal pressures that lead to discouragement. Without the right encouragement, navigating holiday gatherings and events can be challenging. However, with the right mindset and tools, we can manage these pressures successfully. Focusing on meaningful connections, wise spending, and creating traditions that honor our values can help us experience the true joy of the holiday season.

Prayer

Father, in the name of Jesus, I pray that You help me navigate challenging times during the holiday seasons. Your Word in 1 Timothy 6:6-8 reminds us that "godliness with contentment is great gain. For we brought nothing into this world, and it is certain we can carry nothing out. And having food and clothing, with these we shall be content." Help me to find contentment in Your provisions and to focus on what truly matters.

Lord, guide me to spend money wisely and to prioritize meaningful time with family, making wonderful connections with people. Protect me from falling into the many traps of society during the holidays that go against Your will. Help me to create new holiday traditions that honor You and reflect Your love.

I pray this prayer in the name of Jesus Christ. Amen.

Twenty-Four

DAY 21: Co-Parenting God's Way

P hilippians 4:8 (NKJV) Finally, brethren, whatever things are true, whatever things are noble, whatever things are just, whatever things are pure, whatever things are lovely, whatever things are of good report, if there is any virtue and if there is anything praiseworthy—meditate on these things

Ephesians 4:3 (NKJV) Endeavoring to keep the unity of the Spirit in the bond of peace.

Matthew 18:21-22 (NKJV) Then Peter came to Him and said, "Lord, how often shall my brother sin against me, and I forgive him? Up to seven times? Jesus said to him, I do not say to you, up to seven times, but up to seventy times seven.

My Understanding of This Journey

The success of co-parenting depends on you and your child's other parent. The children have very little to do with the success of co-parenting, therefore it's imperative that you are mature and have a strong support system. Focus on the needs of your children above your wants and desires that may not always serve your children. If you have rules for your child in your home that don't apply when your child is with the other parent or guardian, it's your duty to sit down with the other parent or guardian to discuss how to find a solution that is most beneficial for the child. You'll need help from a neutral party such as a pastor or biblical counselor or even a parental coach. Focus on controlling your emotions, speak life over the other parent in front of your child, forgive and forgive again. Give grace to the other parent and communicate effectively. Seek guidance always from God and your support system.

Lesson Learned

Keep your children's other parent in prayer. Keep your children's family in prayer. Control yourself and ask God to handle your thoughts and emotions. REST. Stay active in your relationship with God. Forgive yourself. Set clear and healthy boundaries for you and your children. Keep your support system close and God even closer.

Reflection

Lesson Learned: Pray! Ask God for help. Keep your children, their other parent, and their family in prayer. Control yourself and ask God to manage your thoughts and emotions. REST. Stay active in your relationship with God. Forgive yourself. Set clear and healthy boundaries for you and your children. Keep your support system close and God even closer.

Prayer

Dear Lord, I come before You with a humble heart, seeking Your presence and guidance. Your Word in Philippians 4:8 reminds us to meditate on things that are true, noble, just, pure, lovely, and of good report. Lord, help me to focus my thoughts on these virtues and fill my mind with what is praiseworthy. Let my thoughts be aligned with Your will, and may they bring peace and clarity to my life.

In Ephesians 4:3, You call us to endeavor to keep the unity of the Spirit in the bond of peace. Lord, I pray for unity and peace in my family and relationships. Help me to be a peacemaker, fostering harmony and understanding among those around me. Let Your Spirit guide me in maintaining the bond of peace, even in challenging times.

As I reflect on Matthew 18:21-22, where Peter asked how often he should forgive, and Jesus replied to forgive up to seventy times seven, I am reminded of the boundless grace You offer us. Lord, grant me a forgiving heart. Help me to extend the same grace and forgiveness to others that You have shown me. Let me not hold onto grudges or past hurts but release them to You, finding freedom and peace in forgiveness.

Lord, I need You in every aspect of my life, especially as a parent. Help me to be the best parent I can be for You and my child. Give me patience, wisdom, peace, grace, provision, and the resources to maintain a healthy and balanced life as a parent. Guide me in teaching my child Your ways and nurturing their faith and character.

Thank You, Lord, for Your unwavering love and support. I trust in Your guidance and lean on Your strength. Let my life be a testament to Your grace and mercy, and may I always strive to honor You in all that I do. I pray this prayer in Jesus Christ's name. Amen.

Twenty-Five

Day 22: To Whom Much Is Given

L uke 12:48 (NKJV) But he who did not know, yet committed things deserving of stripes, shall be beaten with few. For everyone to whom much is given, from him much will be required; and to whom much has been committed, of him they will ask the more.

My Understanding of This Journey

Career and work can become demanding at times. Without maintaining a healthy balance, it's going to be difficult to successfully manage the responsibility of being a parent and while working in your career. The good news is that you have opportunities to establish what your limits are with your career endeavors. Consider working with a career coach to help you navigate your ambitions and plans for your career future. God is your provider so as your child's needs change year after year, think about how your career will allow you the time you need to be there for your child while being able to work. Consider exploring career opportunities that offer more flexibility when possible.

Lesson Learned

It's helpful to prepare early by assessing what your daily responsibilities are and organizing your schedule accordingly. Always be aware of the commitments that you want to keep. You want to keep your commitments of course to your child but always acknowledge the commitments that you're keeping in every other part of your life and that includes your career. Tell your employer early and often about your family obligations. Pray and ask the Lord to help you create a healthy balance with maintaining schedules for work, your children and for yourself. Always take time to rest. Call on your support system when you need to.

Reflection

It's helpful to prepare early by assessing your daily responsibilities and organizing your schedule accordingly. Be aware of the commitments you want to keep, especially to your child, but also acknowledge commitments in other areas of your life, including your career. Communicate your family obligations to your employer early and often. Pray and ask the Lord to help you create a healthy balance between work, your children, and yourself. Always take time to rest and call on your support system when needed.

Prayer

Dear Lord, I need You and I trust You. Help me to be a good parent while maintaining a career that honors You and my family. I thank You for providing for me and my family and for protecting my home. Teach me how to keep my commitments while trusting in You. Strengthen me with Your patience, wisdom, and courage.

Thank You, Lord. In Jesus Christ's name, I pray. Amen.

Twenty-Six

DAY 23: Am I a Good Parent?

P salms 55:22 (NKJV) Cast your burden on the Lord, And He shall sustain you; He shall never permit the righteous to be moved."

Proverbs 18:21 (NKJV) Death and life are in the power of the tongue, and those who love it will eat its fruit.

My Understanding of This Journey

There is a difference between wanting what's best for your child and what YOU think is best for your child. When you learn the difference, you'll see that what you want for your child for the most part will be to take care of what your child needs based on your experiences. The question shouldn't focus on a scale of Good and Bad, the goal is to commit to learning what is best for your child and learning how your child will receive health benefits from your decisions from your parenting. No one can raise a child alone, even single parents need help from family, healthcare providers, educators, trusted pastors and spiritual counselors. I say all of this to say that you may not always give your child what they "want" but you can communicate why you're more focused on what they need. Ask God to help you always. I've asked myself this question and the truth is, I try to be a good parent. I try every day. I'm blessed that I have God to help me!

Lesson Learned

To be a parent that gives their child everything the child wants isn't healthy and can have negative consequences later. Stay in prayer and pray for everything concerning you and your children. Give yourself grace! There will always be moments that you will make mistakes, the key is to learn from them! Communicate with your child and spend as much time as you can with them and keep your trusted community and family members close to help you. Don't fall into the trap of guilt or shame, keep moving because you're growing with your child! God sees you and He's with you.

Reflection

Understanding the difference between what's best for your child and what YOU think is best is crucial. Focus on learning what benefits your child's needs rather than just fulfilling their wants. Parenting requires support from family, healthcare providers, educators, and spiritual counselors. Communicate to your child because their needs come first and seek God's guidance. I often ask myself if I am a good parent. The truth is, I try every day, and I am blessed to have God's help in this journey.

Prayer

Dear Lord, Thank You for allowing me to be a parent. I pray that You will protect me on this journey. Give me Your courage to focus on You when times are challenging. Grant me wisdom as I strive to be a good parent each day. Your Word in Psalms 55:22 reminds me to cast my burdens on You, and You shall sustain me; You shall never permit the righteous to be moved. I surrender all my cares and concerns to You, Lord.

Proverbs 18:21 teaches that "Death and life are in the power of the tongue, and those who love it will eat its fruit." Help me to speak life and encouragement into my child's life and into my own. Thank You for Your guidance, blessings, and grace. Strengthen me and the community around me as we navigate the journey of parenthood together. Thank You for Your blessings and love.

In Jesus Christ's name, I pray. Amen.

Twenty-Seven

DAY 24: Am I doing the Right Things ?

P salms 34:4-5 (NKJV) I sought the Lord, and He heard me, And delivered me from all my fears. They looked to Him and were radiant, And their faces were not ashamed."

Proverbs 11:2 (NKJV) When pride comes, then comes shame; But with the humble is wisdom."

My Understanding of This Journey

Over the years I recall not receiving a lot of grace as a parent. I experienced more of the opposite! I was the target of receiving unsolicited advice quite often. I understood that I was learning so much day by day. Each day brought a new challenge, and I tried my best to make sure everything was ok. The problem was, I tried my best. I learned that I operated on my own strength, and it wasn't until I began to see that it's not a question about if I am doing the right things for my child, I discovered I needed to shift my priorities to learn about what God wants me to do for my children. When I began to release doing things on my own, I realized that God did so much for my children. My children are God's children first and He was the best for them. Although I didn't experience a lot of grace in the world, I had an abundant amount of grace from God. Grace can be a beautiful thing when parenting.

Lesson Learned

Be kind to yourself. Give yourself grace. Learn that humility is one of the best ways to learn how to become better at anything. Don't always focus on doing everything right because it's impossible no one can do everything right all the time. focus on being consistent and depending on God to help you. Always ask God for help first. It's okay to receive advice from those that are willing to give it. Remember, you control what advice you want to follow, and you don't have to follow all of it! You and your child are unique! Trust God to guide you and your community to support you to make wise decisions. You control what you put into practice so ask God to give you discernment and make sure that you keep your trusted community and family near so that you can talk through concerns or challenges.

Reflection

Always ask God for help first. It's okay to receive advice from those willing to give it, but remember, you control what advice you want to follow, and you don't have to follow all of it. You and your child are unique! Trust God to guide you and your community to support you in making wise decisions. You control what you put into practice, so ask God for discernment and keep your trusted community and family near to discuss concerns or challenges.

Prayer

Dear Lord Jesus, I thank You, God. I pray that You help me to see Your way of doing things over and above my own ways. I trust You, Lord. I trust Your plan, Your ways, and that You know what's best for more than I could ever know. I trust that You know what's best for my children.

I pray that You will increase my ability to become humbler and more dependent on You. Show me what true humility is so that I may learn that You are my source for every solution. Help me, Lord, to trust You more and to teach my children the importance of trusting You as well.

Thank You, Father, for always being with me. I pray in Jesus Christ's name.

Amen.

Twenty-Eight

DAY 25: For I know the thoughts

Psalms 139:13 (NKJV) For You formed my inward parts; You covered me in my mother's womb.

Jeremiah 29:11 (NKJV) For I know the thoughts that I think toward you, says the LORD, thoughts of peace and not of evil, to give you a future and a hope.

Proverbs (22:6) (NKJV) Train up a child in the way he should go, And when he is old he will not depart from it.

My Understanding of This Journey

If you ask any loving parent what they see in their children, be prepared to hear and witness them give many warmhearted responses about their child. As I watched my children, I noticed great character traits about them. My children spend time with family so of course, my family can give their responses about what they see in my children. The same goes for my children's teachers, their friends, church leaders and just about anyone that spends time with my children can describe the personality and/or character traits of my children. What I see in my children goes beyond what I can physically see. I know that God has a special anointing on my children. Anointed means to consecrate or make sacred and to be set apart. God loves all His children, and His word says so. God has a plan for a bright future for His children. When I realized how God deeply loves His children, it was very reassuring, and it changed how I parent my children.

Only God can see how awesome His children really are and I asked for God's help to support and encourage them. I made many mistakes in parenting, but I always knew that no one or nothing could ever take away my children's anointing from God.

Lesson Learned

I learned that I have a very important responsibility as a parent. I have a responsibility to raise my children to be good, a blessing to others, successful and responsible adults. I also have a responsibility to teach my children about biblical principles as they apply to every facet and season of life. The world can also show my children how to live successfully but I quickly learned that the ways of the world are not the same as God's ways. I only want God's best for my children.

Reflection

I learned that I have a very important responsibility as a parent. It's my duty to raise my children to be good, a blessing to others, successful, and responsible adults. Moreover, I must teach them biblical principles that apply to every facet and season of life. While the world can also show my children how to live successfully, I quickly realized that the ways of the world differ from God's ways. I only want God's best for my child.

Prayer

Dear Lord, I come before You with a heart full of gratitude and humility, acknowledging Your great love and care for us. Your Word in Psalms 139:13 reminds us, "For You formed my inward parts; You covered me in my mother's womb." I am in awe of Your intricate and loving creation, and I thank You for the gift of my child, whom You have wonderfully made.

Lord, Your promise in Jeremiah 29:11 gives me hope and assurance: "For

I know the thoughts that I think toward you, says the LORD, thoughts of peace and not of evil, to give you a future and a hope." I trust in Your good plans for my child's future, plans that are filled with peace and hope. Help me to guide my child according to Your will, encouraging them to walk in the path You have set for them.

Proverbs 22:6 teaches us to "Train up a child in the way he should go, and when he is old, he will not depart from it." I pray for Your wisdom and guidance in raising my child. Help me to instill values of love, kindness, and righteousness in them. May they grow to be a person who honors You in all they do.

Lord, I ask that You fight for my child's peace, wisdom, and strength. Grant them discernment to recognize and resist forces that are not from You. Keep my child safe under Your protective covering. Help them to be loving and kind and teach them to stand firm against sin. Remind my child of their victory and freedom in Christ and let them walk in the confidence of Your love and grace.

Thank You, Father, for always being with us and for Your endless blessings. I place my child in Your hands, trusting that You will guide, protect, and nurture them. I pray all these things in the precious name of Jesus Christ. Amen.

Twenty-Nine

DAY 26: Making Wise the Simple

⸙

salms 19:7-11 (NKJV) "The law of the LORD is perfect, converting the soul; The testimony of the LORD is sure, making wise the simple; The statutes of the LORD are right, rejoicing the heart; The commandment of the LORD is pure, enlightening the eyes; The fear of the LORD is clean, enduring forever; The judgments of the LORD are true and righteous altogether. More to be desired are they then gold, Yea, than much fine gold, Sweeter also than honey and the honeycomb. Moreover, by them Your servant is warned, and in keeping them there is great reward."

My Understanding of This Journey

In the context of dating, it is important to approach this aspect of life with the same wisdom and discernment that Psalms 19:7-11 advocates. Dating should not be taken into consideration unless you know you are ready. This involves asking yourself crucial questions: Am I ready to date? What do I want the result to be? Am I healthy enough to date? Am I ready to tell my children that I want to date? These questions help ensure that you are prepared emotionally, mentally, and spiritually.

Moreover, ensuring that you are healthy enough to date means reflecting on your emotional and mental state. Are you in a place where you can invest in a relationship without compromising your well-being or the well-being of your children? Transparency with your children about your intentions is also essential, as it fosters an environment of trust and understanding. Always seek God's guidance in this journey, praying for wisdom and clarity as you navigate the complexities of dating. Trust in His plan and timing, knowing that adhering to His commandments will lead to a rewarding and fulfilling path.

Lesson Learned

I learned that I needed God to determine if I was ready to date. When I was confused, unhealthy and not ready to date (but I dated anyway), I experienced unsuccessful moments that probably could've been avoided had I consulted with God first. I won't make that mistake again! I learned foundational biblical principles such as forgiveness, getting healed from my past hurts, finding strength in God helped me to date successfully and most importantly, learn how to have healthy relationships.

Reflection

Dating should only be considered when you know you're ready. Important questions to ask yourself include: Am I ready to date? What do I want the end result to be? Am I healthy enough to date? Am I prepared to discuss dating with my children? These questions help ensure that you enter the dating world with clarity, purpose, and the readiness to embrace the journey ahead.

Prayer

Dear Lord, I trust you. I pray that you help learn how to date successfully when the time is right. Lord, I trust your timing. I pray that you help me to become healthy in all areas of my life. I pray that you help me to honor you, honor my children and honor myself as I continue to seek you for help when it comes to dating.

Thank you, Lord, for helping me. I say this prayer in Jesus Christ name amen.

Thirty

DAY 27: Your Ability to Love

E phesians 5:1-5 "Therefore be imitators of God as dear children. And walk in love, as Christ also has loved us and given Himself for us, an offering and a sacrifice to God for a sweet-smelling aroma. But fornication and all uncleanness or covetousness, let it not even be named among you, as is fitting for saints; neither filthiness, nor foolish talking, nor coarse jesting, which are not fitting, but rather giving of thanks. For this you know that no fornicator, unclean person, nor covetous man, who is an idolater, has any inheritance in the kingdom of Christ and God."

My Understanding of This Journey

Without God, I have a limited ability to love. When I didn't walk with the Lord, my ability to love was transactional and conditional. I didn't understand any other way to love until I began my relationship with God. Without God, it's easy to confuse love with other things that inhibit your ability to love such as infatuation, lust, selfishness, idolatry, and pride. God calls us to love like Jesus, love others as we love ourselves and to walk in love. We need God to love the way we're called to love.

Lesson Learned

Without love, you cannot walk or be in the will of God. Without love, you cannot keep God's commandments, and two most important commandments are to love God and the second is to love others. To love is the greatest focus we have in life.

Reflection

Reflecting on this, love is essential in our relationship with God and others. Jesus emphasized love in the greatest commandments: "Love the Lord your God" and "Love your neighbor as yourself." By making love our focus, we fulfill God's will and reflect His nature. In a world of division, choosing love bridges gaps and heals wounds, allowing us to walk in God's will and positively impact others.

Prayer

Dear Lord, I come before You today, seeking Your guidance and strength. Your Word in Ephesians 5:1-5 calls us to be imitators of You, walking in love as Christ has loved us and given Himself for us as an offering and a sacrifice to You, a sweet-smelling aroma. Lord, help me to embody this kind of love in my daily life. Teach me to love as Christ loved, selflessly and sacrificially. Let my actions, words, and thoughts reflect Your love and grace. Remove from me any trace of fornication, uncleanness, or covetousness, as these are not fitting for Your saints. Help me to avoid filthiness, foolish talking, and coarse jesting, which are not suitable, but instead, let me be filled with thanksgiving.

Lord, I understand that no fornicator, unclean person, or covetous man, who is an idolater, has any inheritance in Your kingdom. Therefore, purify my heart and mind, and fill me with Your Holy Spirit so that I may live a life that is pleasing to You. Thank You for Your love, faithfulness, grace, and mercy as I learn to love in the way You want me to. Guide me to walk in love, just as Christ loved us and gave Himself up for us. Strengthen me to be an example of Your love to those around me.

Help me to love my family, friends, and even strangers with the love of Christ. Let Your love shine through me, drawing others closer to You. Teach me to forgive as You forgive, to show compassion as You show compassion, and to serve as You serve. Thank You, Lord, for Your unending love and for the sacrifice of Jesus Christ. May my life be a reflection of Your love and may it be a sweet-smelling aroma to You.

I pray all these things in the precious name of Jesus Christ. Amen.

Thirty-One

DAY 28: Intimacy and Dating

Proverbs 11:14 (NKJV): Where there is no counsel, the people fall; But in the multitude of counselors there is safety.

I Corinthians 6:18 (NKJV) Flee sexual immorality. Every sin that a man does is outside the body, but he who commits sexual immorality sins against his own body.

James 4:17 (NKJV) A man without self-control is like a city broken into and left without walls.

Proverbs 25:28 (ESV) Therefore, to him who knows to do good and does not do it, to him it is sin.

My Understanding of This Journey

I failed in dating without God. My understanding is that the only way to obtain the best results when dating is to date according to biblical principles. Wisdom, maturity, having good spiritual and emotional health are important before starting any dating journey. Intimacy must include clear boundaries.

What does intimacy mean? Intimacy can include physical affection and spending alone time with someone.

Lesson Learned

Honor God in all that you do and honor yourself. You must have clear boundaries and get the help of accountability partners if you start dating. Without boundaries, you are going to fight against your flesh and most people lose the fight. Sex was created for marriage. I understand that sex outside of marriage opens the door for the enemy to come in and cause problems (think roller coaster emotions of guilt, shame and lack of discipline).

Reflection

Establish clear boundaries and seek accountability partners when you start dating. Without boundaries, you risk fighting against your flesh and often losing that battle. By honoring God and setting boundaries, you protect your heart and maintain integrity in your relationships.

Prayer

Dear Lord Jesus, I come before You today, seeking Your guidance, strength, and wisdom. Your Word in Proverbs 11:14 tells us, "Where there is no counsel, the people fall; But in the multitude of counselors there is safety." Lord, I pray for wise counsel and accountability partners who can support and guide me in my journey, especially when it comes to dating and relationships.

In 1 Corinthians 6:18, You command us to "Flee sexual immorality. Every sin that a man does is outside the body, but he who commits sexual immorality sins against his own body." Help me, Lord, to have the discipline and self-control to maintain purity in my mind and body. Strengthen my resolve to honor You in all my actions and decisions.

James 4:17 reminds us, "A man without self-control is like a city broken into and left without walls." Lord, I ask for Your help in building and maintaining strong walls of self-control and discipline in my life. Let Your Holy Spirit guide me and give me the strength to resist temptations that may come my way.

Your Word in Proverbs 25:28 says, "Therefore, to him who knows to do good and does not do it, to him it is sin." Help me, Lord, to always choose to do good and to follow Your commandments. Give me the wisdom to make decisions that are healthy and honoring to You.

Lord, I pray for purity in my thoughts, words, and actions. Help me to keep my mind focused on things that are true, noble, right, pure, lovely, and admirable. Surround me with people who will uplift and encourage me to stay on the path of righteousness. Thank You, Lord, for Your unending love and grace. Thank You for always being with me and guiding me. I trust in Your plan for my life and ask that You continue to lead me in the way everlasting.

In Jesus Christ's name, I pray. Amen.

Thirty-Two

Part IV: Divorced, Separated and Healed

N
o one gets married with the thought of being divorced. At least, that shouldn't be the mindset. However, too often, it becomes a reality for many. It is not a place that anyone wants to be, but it provides a unique perspective on the stages of life—being single, married, and divorced. The journey through these stages involves a whirlwind of thoughts, feelings, and emotions, each challenging in its own way. It is a journey marked by profound transformation, moments of pain, sorrow, and of healing, forgiveness, and grace.

Welcome to my prayer journal, a sacred space where I pour out my heart to God amidst the challenges and blessings of life after divorce. My journey has been one of profound transformation, marked by moments of pain, sorrow, but also of healing, forgiveness, and grace. In these pages, I invite you to join me as I navigate the complexities of divorce, seeking solace and guidance in the comforting embrace of God's love.

The journey of divorce often begins with a profound sense of betrayal and hurt. Yet, as I walk this path, I am reminded of the power of forgiveness. Through prayer and reflection, I am learning to release the burden of resentment and anger, extending grace to myself and my former partner. In the stillness of prayer, I find the strength to forgive, knowing that forgiveness is not only for others but also for my own healing. The pain can be more devastating due to factors like children and the separation of families, but there is grace, love, and peace in God. This is part of our journey in being separated and single after a failed marriage.

Divorce demands a willingness to let go of the life I once knew—a life intertwined with another's. Through prayer, I surrender my grip on the past, releasing my hopes and dreams into God's capable hands. As I let go of control, I discover a newfound freedom in trusting God's plan for my life, knowing that His ways are higher than mine. As a parent navigating divorce, my heart aches for the well-being of my children. In prayer, I bring their hopes, fears, and joys before the throne of grace, trusting that God holds them in the palm of His hand. I seek wisdom and discernment as I strive to nurture and protect them amidst the challenges of separation, knowing that God's love surrounds them always.

For me, it was the sadness of letting go of the family that I had grown to love. The separation of families brings a profound sense of loss and grief. Yet, in the midst of this pain, I cling to the promise of God's faithfulness. Through prayer, I find solace in knowing that God is close to the broken-hearted, binding up our wounds and restoring what has been lost. As I journey through the wilderness of divorce, I am comforted by the knowledge that God walks beside me, guiding me through the valleys and leading me to green pastures.

True healing after divorce comes not from worldly pursuits but from a deep, abiding relationship with God. In prayer, I surrender my brokenness and allow God to mend the pieces of my shattered heart. His healing touch brings restoration and wholeness, transforming my pain into a testimony of His faithfulness. As I place my trust in God's healing power, I embrace the journey towards peace and joy, knowing that He makes all things new. Amidst the chaos and upheaval of divorce, I yearn for inner peace—a peace that surpasses understanding. Through my prayers, I seek refuge in the arms of the Prince of Peace, trusting in His promise to guard my heart and mind. In surrendering my worries and fears to God, I find a sense of calm and serenity that transcends my circumstances.

In the midst of brokenness, I am enveloped by God's unending grace. His love knows no bounds, reaching into the darkest corners of my soul with arms open wide. Through prayer, I am reminded that I am worthy of love and redemption, despite my shortcomings and failures. God's grace sustains me, empowering me to embrace my journey with courage and hope. So, walk with us as we come together in New Kingdom Focus for the healing process.

Divorce demands a willingness to let go of the life I once knew—a life intertwined with another's. Through a relationship with God, prayer, and worship, it is possible to surrender your grip on the past, releasing hopes and dreams into God's capable hands. True healing after divorce comes not from worldly pursuits but from a deep, abiding relationship with God. So, walk with us as we come together in New Kingdom Focus for the healing process.

Scriptural Guidance:

- **Psalm 6:6-7 (NLT)** - "I am worn out from sobbing. All night I flood my bed with weeping, drenching it with my tears. My vision is blurred by grief; my eyes are worn out because of all my enemies."
- **Psalm 147:3 (NLT)** - "He heals the brokenhearted and bandages their wounds."
- **Jeremiah 30:17 (NKJV)** - "For I will restore you to health And I will heal you of your wounds," declares the Lord, "Because they have called you an outcast, saying: 'It is Zion; no one cares for her.'"
- **Jeremiah 33:6 (NKJV)** - "Behold, I will bring to it health and healing, and I will heal them; and I will reveal to them an abundance of peace and truth."

Kingdom Activities for Healing and Restoration:

- **Daily Devotional Readings and Reflections:** Spend time each day reading scripture and reflecting on its application to your life. Allow God's word to comfort and guide you through this period of transformation.

- **Prayer Journaling:** Dedicate a specific time each day to write down your prayers, thoughts, and feelings. This practice helps you to process emotions and seek God's guidance.

- **Group Bible Study:** Join or form a support group with others who are also navigating through similar experiences. Studying the Bible together can provide mutual support and deeper insights.

- **Service and Outreach:** Engage in activities that serve others. Volunteering can shift your focus from personal pain to helping others, which can be healing and rewarding.

- **Worship and Praise:** Participate in regular worship services, singing, and praising God. Music and communal worship can be uplifting and bring you closer to God.

- **Christian Counseling:** Seek professional counseling that is rooted in Christian principles. A counselor can provide practical advice and spiritual support tailored to your journey.

- **Physical Activity:** Incorporate physical exercise into your routine. Activities like walking, yoga, or sports can help manage stress and improve overall well-being.

- **Creative Expression:** Explore creative outlets such as painting, writing, or music. Expressing your emotions through art can be therapeutic and a way to connect with God's creativity.

- **Nature Walks and Meditation:** Spend time in nature, meditating on God's creation. This can provide a peaceful environment for reflection and prayer.

- **Forgiveness Workshops:** Participate in workshops focused on forgiveness. Learning to forgive yourself and others is crucial for healing and moving forward. **Scripture Memorization:** Commit to memorizing key scriptures that speak to your heart. Reciting these verses can provide comfort and strength in difficult moments.

- **Healing Retreats:** Attend retreats designed for healing and spiritual renewal. These can offer concentrated time for reflection, prayer, and fellowship.

Thirty-Three

DAY 29: All Cried Out

P salm 6:6-7 (NLT) I am worn out from sobbing. All night I flood my bed with weeping, drenching it with my tears. My vision is blurred by grief; my eyes are worn out because of all my enemies."

Psalm 147:3 (NLT) He heals the brokenhearted and bandages their wounds."

My Understanding of This Journey

I am worn out from sobbing. All night I flood my bed with weeping, drenching it with my tears. My vision is blurred by grief; my eyes are worn out because of all my enemies. The end of my marriage or long-term relationship is often accompanied by a profound sense of loss and grief. I take time to reflect on the emotions I am experiencing and how they manifest in my life. I allow myself to feel and process these emotions without judgment or rush. I write about the stages of grief I am experiencing, such as denial, anger, bargaining, depression, and acceptance. I reflect on how each stage impacts my thoughts, behaviors, and overall well-being.

Psalm 147:3, "He heals the brokenhearted and bandages their wounds." (NLT). I consider the rituals or practices that help me cope with grief and honor the memory of my relationship. This might include journaling, talking to a therapist or support group, creating a memorial, or engaging in activities that bring me comfort and solace. I reflect on the importance of self-care during this time and the ways in which I prioritize my emotional, mental, and physical well-being. I write about the moments of healing and growth that emerge from allowing myself to grieve fully and authentically.

Lesson Learned

I think about the support systems and resources available to me as I navigate through grief. I reflect on the importance of reaching out to friends, family, or professionals for support and guidance. I consider how their presence and compassion help me feel less alone in my journey. I write about the lessons I learn about myself and my capacity for resilience as I move through the grieving process. By documenting these reflections, I honor the complexity of my emotions and the depth of my experience as I heal from the loss of my relationship or marriage.

Reflection

Grieving the end of a relationship or marriage is a natural and necessary process. How do you cope with the emotions that come with this loss? What strategies help you navigate through grief? Write about your experiences and feelings as you grieve the end of your marriage or relationship.

Prayer

Heavenly Father, I am worn out from sobbing. All night I flood my bed with weeping, drenching it with my tears. My vision is blurred by grief; my eyes are worn out because of all my enemies (Psalm 6:6-7). In the midst of the storm of divorce, I turn to You as my refuge and strength. Grant me the grace to forgive, the peace that surpasses understanding, and the wisdom to let go of the past. Guide me as I care for my children and navigate the challenges of separation, knowing that You are with me every step of the way.

Heavenly Father, you heal the brokenhearted and bandage their wounds (Psalm 147:3). Heal my brokenness and restore my soul, Lord, that I may find peace and joy in Your loving embrace. Amen.

Thirty-Four

DAY 30: Stepping into My Healing

Jeremiah 30:17 (ESV) For I will restore you to health And I will heal you of your wounds,' declares the Lord, 'Because they have called you an outcast, saying: "It is Zion; no one cares for her.

Jeremiah 33:6 (ESV) Behold, I will bring to it health and healing, and I will heal them; and I will reveal to them an abundance of peace and truth.

My Understanding of This Journey

Jeremiah 30:17 'For I will restore you to health And I will heal you of your wounds,' declares the Lord, 'Because they have called you an outcast, saying: "It is Zion; no one cares for her."' In times of heartache and pain, turning to my faith provides me with comfort and strength. I reflect on my relationship with God and the ways in which I lean on Him for healing and guidance. Prayer, meditation, scripture reading, and attending religious services help me connect with God's presence and find solace in His love. I write about the moments of divine intervention and grace that bring me peace and comfort as I navigate through the challenges of divorce or separation.

Jeremiah 33:6 Behold, I will bring to it health and healing, and I will heal them; and I will reveal to them an abundance of peace and truth. I think about the ways in which I surrender my pain and burdens to God, trusting in His plan for my life. I reflect on the moments of transformation and renewal that emerge as I allow God to work in my heart and mind. I consider the lessons I learn about trust, surrender, and the power of faith to overcome adversity. I write about the ways in which my relationship with God deepens and strengthens as I lean on Him for healing and restoration.

Lesson Learned

I consider the support systems and resources available to me within my faith community as I seek healing and wholeness. I reflect on the importance of community, fellowship, and spiritual guidance in nurturing my relationship with God. I consider how I can serve and support others who are also experiencing the pain of divorce or separation. I write about the ways in which my faith journey shapes my perspective on healing and resilience, and the hope and comfort I find in God's unfailing love.

Reflection

Reflect on your relationship with God and the role of faith in healing from the pain of divorce or separation. How do you lean on your faith during difficult times? What practices help you connect with God and find solace in His presence? Write about your experiences and feelings as you allow God to heal you.

Prayer

Heavenly Father, I come before You with a heart heavy with burdens, yet hopeful in Your promises. Your Word in Jeremiah 30:17 declares, "For I will restore you to health and I will heal you of your wounds," because they have called me an outcast. Lord, I trust in Your promise to restore my health and heal my wounds. I pray that You mend the broken places within me and restore me to wholeness.

In Jeremiah 33:6, You proclaim, "Behold, I will bring to it health and healing, and I will heal them; and I will reveal to them an abundance of peace and truth." Lord, I ask for Your healing touch to bring health and healing to every aspect of my life. Reveal to me an abundance of peace and truth, that I may walk in Your light and experience the fullness of Your love and grace.

Thank You, Lord, for Your unfailing love and mercy. I trust in Your plan and Your power to heal and restore. Guide me, protect me, and fill me with Your peace.

In Jesus' name, I pray. Amen.

Thirty-Five

DAY 31: God is My Keeper

1 **Peter 3:15 (NIV)** But in your hearts honor Christ the Lord as holy, always being prepared to make a defense to anyone who asks you for a reason for the hope that is in you; yet do it with gentleness and respect.

1 **Samuel 12:22 (NIV)** For the Lord will not forsake his people, for his great name's sake, because it has pleased the Lord to make you a people for himself.

1 **Samuel 16:7 (NIV)** But the Lord said to Samuel, "Do not look on his appearance or on the height of his stature, because I have rejected him. For the Lord sees not as man sees man looks on the outward appearance, but the Lord looks on the heart.

Colossians 1:2 (NIV) To the saints and faithful brothers in Christ at Colossae: Grace to you and peace from God our Father.

My Understanding of This Journey

For the Lord will not forsake his people, for his great name's sake, because it has pleased the Lord to make you a people for himself. Divorce or separation often brings about a profound sense of loss and upheaval, including the loss of self and identity. I reflect on the ways in which my sense of self has been intertwined with my role as a spouse or partner. I consider the aspects of my identity that I may have compromised or neglected during the relationship. I write about the emotions and challenges that arise as I confront this loss and embark on a journey of self-discovery.

But the Lord said to Samuel, "Do not look on his appearance or on the height of his stature, because I have rejected him. For the Lord sees not as man sees man looks on the outward appearance, but the Lord looks on the heart. "I consider the opportunities for growth and transformation that come with reclaiming my sense of self and identity. I reflect on the values, passions, and interests that define me as an individual. What aspects of my identity bring me joy, fulfillment, and a sense of purpose? I write about the moments of clarity and empowerment as I reconnect with my authentic self and embrace the freedom to explore new possibilities.

Lesson Learned

I think about the support systems and resources available to me as I navigate through this process of self-redefinition. I reflect on the importance of self-care, self-compassion, and self-expression in nurturing my sense of self-worth and belonging. I consider how therapy, journaling, creative outlets, or support groups can help me process my emotions and rediscover my identity. I write about the moments of empowerment and self-discovery that emerge as I embrace my individuality and chart a new path forward. By documenting these reflections, I honor the complexity of my journey and the resilience of my spirit as I rebuild my life after divorce or separation.

Reflection

The end of a marriage or relationship can bring about a loss of self and identity. How do you navigate through this loss? What strategies help you rediscover and reclaim your sense of self? Write about your experiences and feelings as you redefine your identity in the wake of divorce or separation.

Prayer

Heavenly Father, I come before You with a heart full of gratitude and reverence. Your Word in 1 Peter 3:15 instructs us to honor Christ the Lord as holy in our hearts and to always be prepared to make a defense to anyone who asks for the reason for the hope that is in us, doing so with gentleness and respect. Lord, help me to honor You in my heart always and to be ready to share the hope I have in You with others, showing gentleness and respect in all my interactions.

1 Samuel 12:22 reassures us that You will not forsake Your people, for Your great name's sake, because it has pleased You to make us a people for Yourself. Thank You, Lord, for Your unwavering faithfulness and for choosing us to be Your own. May I always remember Your great love and commitment to us.

In 1 Samuel 16:7, You remind us that You do not look on outward appearances, but You look on the heart. Help me to see myself and others through Your eyes, valuing what is in the heart over outward appearances. Guide me to cultivate a heart that is pure and pleasing to You.

Colossians 1:2 greets the saints and faithful brothers in Christ at Colossae with grace and peace from God our Father. Lord, I ask for Your grace and peace to fill my life and the lives of those around me. May we all experience Your love and mercy in abundance. Thank You, Father, for Your continuous guidance and support. Help me to live a life that honors You and reflects Your love and grace to the world.

In Jesus' name, I pray. Amen.

Thirty-Six

DAY 32: Overcoming Internal Struggles

P roverbs 16:32 (ESV) Whoever is slow to anger is better than the mighty, and he who rules his spirit than he who takes a city.

Galatians 5:17 (ESV) For the desires of the flesh are against the Spirit, and the desires of the Spirit are against the flesh, for these are opposed to each other, to keep you from doing the things you want to do'.

Luke 6:45 (ESV) The good person out of the good treasure of his heart produces good, and the evil person out of his evil treasure produces evil, for out of the abundance of the heart his mouth speaks.

Joshua 1:9 (ESV) Have I not commanded you? Be strong and courageous. Do not be frightened, and do not be dismayed, for the Lord your God is with you wherever you go."

My Understanding of This Journey

Galatians 5:17 For the desires of the flesh are against the Spirit, and the desires of the Spirit are against the flesh, for these are opposed to each other, to keep you from doing the things you want to do. Emotions can run high in the wake of divorce or separation, making it essential to develop strategies for regulating and managing overwhelming feelings. I reflect on the emotions I experience and the ways in which they impact my thoughts, behaviors, and relationships. I consider the triggers that exacerbate emotional distress and contribute to feelings of anxiety, sadness, or anger. I write about the moments of insight and awareness as I recognize patterns and identify triggers that undermine my emotional well-being.

Joshua 1:9 Have I not commanded you? Be strong and courageous. Do not be frightened, and do not be dismayed, for the LORD your God is with you wherever you go. I think about the strategies and practices that help me regulate my emotions and maintain a sense of balance and stability. I reflect on the importance of self-care, self-awareness, and self-regulation in nurturing emotional resilience. I consider how mindfulness, relaxation techniques, and healthy coping mechanisms help me navigate through difficult emotions and situations. I write about the moments of empowerment and strength as I take proactive steps to protect my mental and emotional health.

Lesson Learned

I consider the support systems and resources available to me as I learn to regulate my emotions and identify triggers. I reflect on the importance of seeking guidance and support from trusted friends, family, or professionals who can provide insight and encouragement. I consider how my faith and spiritual practices offer a source of comfort and strength as I confront and overcome emotional challenges. I write about the ways in which I cultivate emotional resilience and well-being as I learn to regulate my emotions and navigate through the ups and downs of life after divorce or separation. By documenting these reflections, I honor the complexity of my emotional journey and empower myself to create a future filled with emotional health and vitality.

Reflection

Reflect on the importance of regulating emotions and identifying triggers as you navigate through the emotional aftermath of divorce or separation. How do you manage overwhelming feelings in healthy and constructive ways? What strategies help you recognize and address triggers that exacerbate emotional distress? Write about your experiences and insights as you learn to regulate your emotions and protect your well-being.

Prayer

Heavenly Father, I come before You with a heart full of gratitude and humility, seeking Your guidance and strength. Your Word in Proverbs 16:32 teaches us that whoever is slow to anger is better than the mighty, and he who rules his spirit is greater than he who takes a city. Lord, help me to be slow to anger and to exercise self-control, ruling my spirit with Your wisdom and grace.

In Galatians 5:17, You remind us that the desires of the flesh are against the Spirit, and the desires of the Spirit are against the flesh. These are opposed to each other to keep us from doing the things we want to do. Lord, I pray for the strength to resist the desires of the flesh and to walk in the Spirit, aligning my actions with Your will.

Luke 6:45 teaches us that the good person out of the good treasure of his heart produces good, and the evil person out of his evil treasure produces evil, for out of the abundance of the heart his mouth speaks. Lord, fill my heart with Your goodness and love, so that my words and actions reflect the treasures of a heart devoted to You.

Your command in Joshua 1:9 encourages us to be strong and courageous, to not be frightened or dismayed, for You, Lord, our God, are with us wherever we go. Lord, grant me the courage and strength to face life's challenges, knowing that You are always with me, guiding and protecting me.

Thank You, Father, for Your unwavering presence and for the strength You provide. Help me to live out these principles daily, showing self-control, walking in the Spirit, speaking goodness, and facing challenges with courage. In Jesus' name, I pray. Amen.

Thirty-Seven

DAY 33: Being Restored

Nehemiah 2:18 (ESV) I told them how the hand of my God had been favorable to me and also about the king's words which he had spoken to me. Then they said, "Let us arise and build." So, they put their hands to the good work.

Philippians 4:19 (ESV) And my God will supply every need of yours according to His riches in glory in Christ Jesus.

Matthew 6:13 (ESV) And lead us not into temptation, but deliver us from evil."

Deuteronomy 8:18 (ESV) You shall remember the Lord your God, for it is He who gives you power to get wealth, that He may confirm His covenant that He swore to your fathers, as it is this day.

My Understanding of This Journey

"You shall remember the Lord your God, for it is He who gives you power to get wealth, that He may confirm His covenant that He swore to your fathers, as it is this day" (Deuteronomy 8:18). Divorce or separation often necessitates a period of rebuilding and restructuring various aspects of my life. I reflect on the areas of my life that have been impacted by the end of my relationship, including my career, home, and finances. I consider the opportunities for growth and reinvention that come with starting anew. I write about the steps I am taking to rebuild my life and create a future filled with possibility and abundance.

"And lead us not into temptation, but deliver us from evil" (Matthew 6:13, ESV). I think about the strategies and practices that help me navigate through the challenges of rebuilding my life after divorce or separation. I reflect on the importance of resilience, adaptability, and resourcefulness in overcoming obstacles and setbacks. I consider how setting goals, seeking support, and embracing change contribute to my sense of empowerment and progress. I write about the moments of transformation and renewal as I reclaim control over my life and shape a future that reflects my values and aspirations.

Lesson Learned

I consider the support systems and resources available to me as I rebuild various aspects of my life. I reflect on the importance of seeking guidance and support from trusted friends, family, or professionals who can provide encouragement and assistance. I consider how my faith and spiritual practices offer a source of strength and guidance as I navigate through the complexities of rebuilding. I write about the ways in which I cultivate resilience and determination as I rebuild my life after divorce or separation, and the hope and optimism I hold for the future. By documenting these reflections, I honor the resilience of my spirit and empower myself to create a life filled with purpose and fulfillment.

Reflection

Rebuilding your life after divorce or separation involves a multifaceted process of renewal and transformation. How do you approach rebuilding various aspects of your life, including your career, home, and finances? What strategies help you navigate through these changes with resilience and determination? Write about your experiences and insights as you embark on a journey of rebuilding and renewal.

Prayer

Heavenly Father, I come before You with a heart full of gratitude for Your unwavering support and guidance. As Nehemiah 2:18 reminds us, Your hand has been favorable to me, and with Your words, I am encouraged to rise and build. Lord, help me to put my hands to the good work You have set before me, trusting in Your favor and direction.

In Philippians 4:19, You promise to supply every need of ours according to Your riches in glory in Christ Jesus. Thank You, Lord, for Your abundant provision. I trust in Your promise and rely on Your riches to meet all my needs. Let me always remember that You are my source and provider.

Matthew 6:13 teaches us to pray, "And lead us not into temptation, but deliver us from evil." Father, I ask for Your protection and guidance. Keep me from the paths of temptation and deliver me from all forms of evil. Strengthen my spirit to resist anything that seeks to draw me away from Your will.

Deuteronomy 8:18 reminds us to remember the Lord our God, for it is You who gives us the power to get wealth, that You may confirm Your covenant. Lord, I acknowledge that all my abilities and opportunities come from You. Help me to use them wisely and for Your glory, always remembering to give You thanks and honor.

Thank You, Lord, for Your faithful presence in my life. Guide me, provide for me, protect me, and empower me to do the work You have called me to do. Let all that I do bring glory to Your name.

In Jesus' name, I pray. Amen.

Thirty-Eight

DAY 34: Pressing Forward

P roverbs 4:23 (ESV), it says "Guard your heart above all else, for it determines the course of your life.

2 Peter 1:5–7 (ESV) For this very reason, make every effort to supplement your faith with virtue, and virtue with knowledge, **6** and knowledge with self-control, and self-control with steadfastness, and steadfastness with godliness, 7 and godliness with brotherly affection, and brotherly affection with love.

My Understanding of This Journey
"For this very reason, make every effort to supplement your faith with virtue, and virtue with knowledge, and knowledge with self-control, and self-control with steadfastness, and steadfastness with godliness, and godliness with brotherly affection, and brotherly affection with love." (2 Peter 1:5–7). Entering the dating scene after divorce or separation can evoke a range of emotions and uncertainties. I reflect on my readiness to date and the factors that influence my decision to pursue romantic relationships. I consider the lessons I've learned from past relationships and how they shape my approach to dating. I write about the fears, hopes, and expectations I have as

I contemplate the possibility of opening my heart to love once again.

Guard your heart above all else, for it determines the course of your life." (Proverbs 4:23). I think about the qualities and values I seek in a partner and how they align with my own goals and aspirations. I reflect on the importance of self-awareness, self-care, and self-love in fostering healthy relationships. I consider how taking time to reflect on my needs and desires can help me make informed decisions about dating and romance. I write about the moments of clarity and insight as I explore my readiness and willingness to embark on a new chapter of love and companionship.

Lesson Learned

I consider the support systems and resources available to me as I navigate through this process of self-discovery and exploration. I reflect on the importance of seeking guidance and support from trusted friends, family, or professionals who can offer perspective and encouragement. I consider how my faith and spiritual practices offer a source of wisdom and guidance as I discern my path forward. I write about the ways in which I cultivate self-awareness and confidence as I assess my readiness to date after divorce or separation, and the hope and optimism I hold for the future. By documenting these reflections, I honor the complexity of my journey and empower myself to pursue love and happiness on my own terms.

Reflection

As you move forward from divorce or separation, you may find yourself contemplating the possibility of dating again. How do you assess your readiness to enter the dating scene? What factors influence your decision to pursue romantic relationships? Write about your thoughts and feelings as you consider the prospect of dating after divorce or separation.

Prayer

Heavenly Father, I come before You today with a humble heart, seeking Your wisdom and guidance. Your Word in Proverbs 4:23 instructs us to "Guard your heart above all else, for it determines the course of your life." Lord, help me to guard my heart diligently. Protect it from negative influences and fill it with Your love and truth, guiding my steps and decisions according to Your will.

In 2 Peter 1:5-7, we are encouraged to supplement our faith with virtue, and virtue with knowledge, knowledge with self-control, self-control with steadfastness, steadfastness with godliness, godliness with brotherly affection, and brotherly affection with love. Lord, help me to make every effort to grow in these qualities. Strengthen my faith and let it be reflected in my actions. Fill me with Your wisdom and knowledge. Grant me self-control to resist temptations and steadfastness to remain faithful in my walk with You.

Cultivate godliness within me, so that I may reflect Your character in all that I do. Fill my heart with brotherly affection and love, so that I may treat others with kindness and compassion. Let Your love flow through me, impacting those around me and bringing glory to Your name.

Thank You, Father, for Your continuous guidance and love. Help me to grow in virtue, knowledge, self-control, steadfastness, godliness, brotherly affection, and love. Guard my heart and lead me in the path that honors You.

In Jesus' name, I pray. Amen.

Thirty-Nine

DAY 35: Repairing the Breach

Deuteronomy 3:22 (ESV) You must not fear them, for the Lord your God Himself fights for you."

Isaiah 41:10 (ESV) Fear not, for I am with you; be not dismayed, for I am your God; I will strengthen you, I will help you, I will uphold you with my righteous right hand.

2 Timothy 1:7 (NIV) For God gave us a spirit not of fear but of power and love and self-control."

Joshua 1:9 (NIV) Have I not commanded you? Be strong and courageous. Do not be frightened, and do not be dismayed, for the Lord your God is with you wherever you go.

Isaiah 43:1 (ESV) Fear not, for I have redeemed you; I have called you by name, you are mine.

My Understanding of This Journey

"Fear not, for I have redeemed you; I have called you by name, you are mine." (Isaiah 43:1). Fear has the power to paralyze me and prevent me from moving forward after divorce or separation. I reflect on the fears that hold me back and the ways in which they manifest in my thoughts and behaviors. I consider the impact of fear on my ability to embrace change, take risks, and pursue new opportunities. I write about the moments of vulnerability and courage as I confront my fears and reclaim control over my life.

"Fear not, for I am with you; be not dismayed, for I am your God; I will strengthen you, I will help you, I will uphold you with my righteous right hand." (Isaiah 41:10). "For God gave us a spirit not of fear but of power and love and self-control." (2 Timothy 1:7). I think about the strategies and practices that help me confront and overcome my fears. I reflect on the importance of self-awareness, self-compassion, and self-empowerment in building resilience and confidence. I consider how reframing negative beliefs, setting boundaries, and taking small steps outside my comfort zone contribute to my personal growth and development. I write about the moments of triumph and empowerment as I confront and conquer my fears, and the sense of liberation and empowerment that comes from embracing life with courage and resilience. I consider the support systems and resources available to me as I navigate through this process of confronting and overcoming fear. I reflect on the importance of seeking guidance and support from trusted friends, family, or professionals who can offer encouragement and perspective.

Lesson Learned

I consider how my faith and spiritual practices offer a source of strength and guidance as I confront my fears and embrace new possibilities. I write about the ways in which I cultivate courage and resilience as I confront and conquer my fears, and the hope and optimism I hold for the future. By documenting these reflections,

I honor the bravery of my spirit and empower myself to live a life filled with courage and purpose. Isaiah 43:1 "Fear not, for I have redeemed you; I have called you by name, you are mine."

Reflection

Fear can be a significant barrier to moving forward after divorce or separation. How do you confront and overcome your fears as you navigate through life's challenges? What strategies help you cultivate courage and resilience in the face of uncertainty? Write about your experiences and insights as you confront and conquer your fears.

Prayer

Heavenly Father, I come before You with a heart seeking Your strength and guidance. Your Word in Deuteronomy 3:22 reassures us, "You must not fear them, for the Lord your God Himself fights for you." Lord, help me to remember that You are always fighting for me, and there is no need for fear when You are by my side.

Isaiah 41:10 reminds us, "Fear not, for I am with you; be not dismayed, for I am your God; I will strengthen you, I will help you, I will uphold you with my righteous right hand." Lord, I thank You for Your presence in my life. Strengthen me, help me, and uphold me with Your righteous right hand. Let me find comfort and courage in knowing that You are always with me.

In 2 Timothy 1:7, You tell us, "For God gave us a spirit not of fear but of power and love and self-control." Lord, fill me with Your spirit of power, love, and self-control. Remove any fear from my heart and replace it with Your strength and love.

Joshua 1:9 commands us to "Be strong and courageous. Do not be frightened, and do not be dismayed, for the Lord your God is with you wherever you go." Lord, grant me the courage to face every challenge with confidence, knowing that You are with me wherever I go. Help me to be strong and fearless, trusting in Your constant presence and guidance.

Isaiah 43:1 declares, "Fear not, for I have redeemed you; I have called you by name, you are mine." Lord, I am grateful for Your redemption and for calling me by name. I am Yours, and in this truth, I find peace and security.

Thank You, Father, for Your promises and for Your unwavering presence in my life. Help me to live fearlessly, empowered by Your love and strength.

In Jesus' name, I pray. Amen.

Forty

DAY 36: Capacity to Love and Heal

❧❧❧

1 John 4:19 (NIV) We love because he first loved us.

Galatians 5:22-23 (NLT) But the Holy Spirit produces this kind of fruit in our lives: love, joy, peace, patience, kindness, goodness, faithfulness, gentleness, and self-control. There is no law against these things!

Timothy 1:7 (NLT) For God has not given us a spirit of fear and timidity, but of power, love, and self-discipline.

My Understanding of This Journey

We love because he first loved us." (1 John 4:19 NIV). Divorce or separation can leave scars on my heart, leading me to question my capacity to love and be loved. I reflect on the doubts and insecurities that arise as I contemplate my worthiness for love. I consider the impact of past experiences on my self-esteem and confidence in forming meaningful relationships. I write about the moments of self-doubt and vulnerability as I grapple with questions of love and worthiness. "But the Holy Spirit produces this kind of fruit in our lives: love, joy, peace, patience, kindness, goodness, faithfulness, gentleness, and self-control. There is no law against these things!" (Galatians 5:22-23

NLT) I think about the strategies and practices that help me cultivate self-love and acceptance.

I reflect on the importance of self-compassion, self-care, and self-awareness in nurturing a positive sense of self-worth. I consider how affirmations, gratitude practices, and acts of kindness toward myself can help me recognize and appreciate my inherent value. I write about the moments of self-discovery and empowerment as I embrace my worthiness for love and connection. "For God has not given us a spirit of fear and timidity, but of power, love, and self-discipline." (2 Timothy 1:7 NLT)

Lesson Learned

I consider the support systems and resources available to me as I explore my capacity for love and connection. I reflect on the importance of seeking guidance and support from trusted friends, family, or professionals who can offer encouragement and perspective. I consider how my faith and spiritual practices offer a source of strength and guidance as I navigate these emotions and experiences. I write about the ways in which I cultivate self-awareness and confidence as I embrace my worthiness for love and connection, and the hope and optimism I hold for the future. By documenting these reflections, I honor the resilience of my spirit and empower myself to pursue love and happiness on my own terms.

Reflection

After divorce or separation, you may question your capacity to love and be loved. How do you overcome doubts and insecurities about your worthiness for love? What strategies help you cultivate self-love and acceptance? Write about your experiences and insights as you explore your capacity for love and connection.

Prayer

Heavenly Father, I come before You with a heart full of gratitude and love. Your Word in 1 John 4:19 reminds us that we love because You first loved us. Lord, thank You for Your unending love, which serves as the foundation of our lives. Help me to love others as You have loved me, showing kindness and compassion in all my interactions.

Galatians 5:22-23 teaches us that the Holy Spirit produces this kind of fruit in our lives: love, joy, peace, patience, kindness, goodness, faithfulness, gentleness, and self-control. Lord, I pray that these fruits will flourish in my life. Fill me with Your Spirit so that I may exhibit love, joy, and peace in abundance. Grant me patience and kindness in dealing with others, and help me to live a life of goodness, faithfulness, gentleness, and self-control.

In 2 Timothy 1:7, You remind us that You have not given us a spirit of fear and timidity, but of power, love, and self-discipline. Lord, strengthen me with Your power and love. Remove any fear or timidity from my heart and fill me with courage and self-discipline. Let Your Spirit guide me in all that I do, empowering me to live boldly for You.

Thank You, Father, for Your love and for the gifts of the Holy Spirit. Help me to live a life that reflects Your love and brings glory to Your name.

In Jesus' name, I pray. Amen.

Forty-One

DAY 37: Making Connections

R omans 5:8 (ESV) God showed His love for us by sending Christ to die for us while we were still sinners.

Hebrews 4:16 (NIV) We can approach God's throne of grace with confidence and receive His mercy and help.

1 Peter 5:7 (ESV) We can cast all our anxiety on God because He cares for us.

1 John 5:2-3 (ESV) We show our love for God and His children by keeping His commandments.

My Understanding of This Journey

In my life, personal scriptures like 1 Peter 5:7 and 1 John 5:2-3 illuminate my path, reminding me of God's unwavering care and love. When I surrender my worries to Him, I feel a tangible relief as He bears my burdens with grace and compassion. Keeping His commandments becomes an expression of my love for Him and His children, fostering unity and harmony within His kingdom. Psalm 23 resonates deeply with me, revealing God's role as my shepherd.

In His guidance, protection, and comfort, I discover solace and strength to confront life's challenges with courage and resilience. Hebrews 4:16 reassures me of His limitless mercy and aid, empowering me to approach His throne of grace with unwavering confidence, knowing He listens and responds to my prayers. For me, faith and spirituality aren't just theoretical concepts; they're living principles that shape my worldview and direct my actions. They offer guidance amidst life's complexities, grounding me in eternal truths that transcend worldly concerns. Living in harmony with my faith brings alignment and fulfillment, enabling me to embody God's love and grace in every aspect of my life.

Community, fellowship, and spiritual guidance are indispensable on my journey of faith. Surrounding myself with fellow believers strengthens my connection with God and provides vital support in times of need. Together, we share in each other's joys and sorrows, lifting one another up as we progress along our individual paths toward spiritual growth and transformation. During moments of trial and uncertainty, my relationship with God serves as an unshakable source of strength and comfort. Through prayer and reflection, I draw nearer to Him, finding solace in His presence and guidance. His peace, surpassing all understanding, calms the storms within my soul and renews my spirit with hope and assurance.

Lesson Learned

Recording these reflections isn't merely an exercise; it's a sacred acknowledgment of the divine presence in my life and a recommitment to spiritual growth and transformation. As I continue forward, I am deeply grateful for the abundant blessings and the profound impact of God's love on my life and well-being.

Reflection

Reflect on the state of your relationship with God. How do you nurture and deepen this relationship in your daily life? What practices or rituals help you feel connected to the divine? Write about your experiences and insights as you explore your spiritual journey and connection with God.

Prayer

Heavenly Father, I come before You with a heart full of gratitude and awe for Your incredible love and grace. Romans 5:8 reminds us that You showed Your love for us by sending Christ to die for us while we were still sinners. Thank You, Lord, for this unimaginable sacrifice and for loving us even when we were unworthy.

In Hebrews 4:16, You invite us to approach Your throne of grace with confidence to receive Your mercy and help. Lord, I come before You boldly, seeking Your mercy and assistance in every aspect of my life. Thank You for being a God who is always accessible and willing to help in our times of need.

1 Peter 5:7 tells us that we can cast all our anxiety on You because You care for us. Father, I lay my worries and anxieties at Your feet, knowing that You care deeply for me. Fill me with Your peace and comfort and help me to trust in Your loving care.

1 John 5:2-3 reminds us that we show our love for You and Your children by keeping Your commandments. Lord, help me to live a life that reflects my love for You through obedience to Your Word. Guide my actions and decisions so that they align with Your will and demonstrate my commitment to Your commandments.

Thank You, Father, for Your endless love, grace, and care. Strengthen my faith and help me to live a life that honors You.

In Jesus' name, I pray. Amen.

Forty-Two

DAY 38: Seek God First

Matthew 6:33 (NIV) But seek first the kingdom of God and his righteousness, and all these things will be added to you.

Matthew 6:6 (NIV) But when you pray, go into your room and shut the door and pray to your Father who is in secret. And your Father who sees in secret will reward you. So, faith comes from hearing, and hearing through the word of Christ.

Psalm 119:105 (NIV) Your word is a lamp to my feet and a light to my path.

My Understanding of This Journey

But when you pray, go into your room and shut the door and pray to your Father who is in secret. And your Father who sees in secret will reward you. So, faith comes from hearing, and hearing through the word of Christ. Prayer is a sacred practice that allows you to commune with the divine and seek guidance, comfort, and solace in times of need. Reflect on the significance of prayer in your spiritual journey and how it shapes your relationship with God. Consider the ways in which you approach prayer as a form of communication, meditation, or contemplation. Reflect on the rituals, traditions, or practices that help you create sacred space for connecting with the divine. Write about the moments of spiritual clarity and divine intervention that come from spending time in prayer and communion with God

But seek first the kingdom of God and his righteousness, and all these things will be added to you. Think about the intentions and desires you bring to your prayers and how they reflect your deepest hopes and aspirations. Reflect on the ways in which prayer helps you cultivate a sense of gratitude, surrender, and trust in the divine plan for your life. Consider how you incorporate prayer into your daily routine and the impact it has on your overall well-being. Write about the moments of transformation and renewal that emerge from seeking divine guidance and support through prayer.

Lesson Learned

Consider the support systems and resources available to you as you deepen your prayer practice and spiritual connection. Reflect on the importance of community, fellowship, and spiritual guidance in nurturing your relationship with God. Consider how your prayers offer a source of strength and comfort in times of trial and uncertainty. Write about the ways in which you cultivate a deeper connection with the divine through prayer and the profound impact it has on your life and spiritual journey. By documenting these reflections, you honor the sacredness of prayer and affirm your commitment to spiritual growth and communion with God.

Reflection

Reflect on the significance of prayer and spending time with God in your spiritual journey. How do you approach prayer as a means of communication with the divine? What practices help you create sacred space for connecting with God? Write about your experiences and insights as you explore the power of prayer and divine communion.

Prayer

Heavenly Father, I come before You in the name of Jesus, seeking Your guidance and help in my dating journey. Your Word in Matthew 6:33 reminds me to seek first the kingdom of God and Your righteousness, knowing that all these things will be added to me. Lord, I want to prioritize Your kingdom and righteousness in all aspects of my life, including dating.

In Matthew 6:6, You instruct us to pray in secret, assuring us that our Father who sees in secret will reward us. Lord, I come to You in the quietness of my heart, asking for Your wisdom and discernment. Help me to be intentional and mindful during this dating process. I trust that You know who You have in store for me, and I desire what You want for my life.

Psalm 119:105 declares that Your Word is a lamp to my feet and a light to my path. Lord, let Your Word guide me in every step I take. Illuminate my path and help me to see what You see and hear what You hear. Keep me aligned with Your will and purpose.

God, I know You have my best interest at heart. Help me to trust in You completely and lean not on my own desires and understanding. Let my actions and decisions be a reflection of my faith in You.

In Jesus' name, I pray. Amen.

Forty-Three

DAY 39: Few are Chosen

G alatians 5:13 (NIV) For you were called to freedom, brothers.
Only do not use your freedom as an opportunity for the flesh, but
through love serve one another.

Romans 12:11 (NIV) Do not be slothful in zeal, be fervent in spirit, serve
the Lord.

My Understanding of This Journey

Your ministry or life's purpose is a sacred calling that invites you to serve
others and make a positive impact in the world. Reflect on the ways in
which you live out this calling in your daily life. Consider the gifts, talents,
and passions that God has bestowed upon you and how you use them to
serve others. Reflect on the ways in which you embody love, compassion,
and empathy in your interactions with others. Write about the moments of
fulfillment and joy that come from aligning your actions with your calling
and mission in life.

Think about the opportunities for growth and transformation that come
from embracing your ministry or life's purpose. Reflect on the challenges
and obstacles you face in fulfilling your calling and how you navigate through

them with faith and determination. Consider how you seek guidance and support from God and others as you pursue your mission in life. Write about the moments of divine inspiration and guidance that affirm your path and empower you to make a difference in the world.

Lesson Learned

Consider the support systems and resources available to you as you live out your ministry or life's purpose. Reflect on the importance of community, fellowship, and spiritual guidance in nurturing your calling and mission. Consider how your faith and spiritual practices offer a source of strength and inspiration as you serve others and make a positive impact in the world. Write about the ways in which you embody your ministry or life's purpose each day and the profound impact it has on your life and the lives of those around you. By documenting these reflections, you honor the sacredness of your calling and affirm your commitment to living a life of purpose and service to God and humanity.

Reflection

Reflect on your ministry or life's purpose and how you live it out each day. How do you serve others and make a positive impact in the world? What gifts and talents do you offer in service to God and humanity? Write about your experiences and insights as you explore your calling and mission in life.

Prayer

Heavenly Father, I come before You with a heart full of gratitude for the freedom You have given us. As Galatians 5:13 reminds us, "For you were called to freedom, brothers. Only do not use your freedom as an opportunity for the flesh, but through love serve one another." Lord, help me to use the freedom You have granted not for selfish desires, but to serve others in love. Teach me to always look for ways to be of service to those around me, reflecting Your love and grace.

Romans 12:11 instructs us, "Do not be slothful in zeal, be fervent in spirit, serve the Lord." Lord, ignite a passion within me to serve You wholeheartedly. Let my spirit be fervent, full of zeal and enthusiasm in serving You and Your kingdom. Help me to avoid laziness and complacency, and to remain diligent and committed to the work You have called me to do.

Lord, guide my actions and my heart to be in alignment with Your will. Fill me with Your Spirit so that I may serve You and others with love, dedication, and joy. Thank You for the freedom and opportunities You have given me. May all that I do bring glory and honor to Your name.

In Jesus' name, I pray. Amen.

Forty-Four

Part V: Dating and Being in Ministry

Wow! This topic right here is a serious matter. Where should we begin? We don't just date to date. Your dating should be intentional. You do not need to go out for someone to feed you. What are you saying about yourself? Save for your own meal. You do not need the attention because all attention is not good attention. If you find that you do need the attention, then it would be good to work on that area to find out why the attention is needed. Why waste time stirring up emotions and potentially falling for someone or having someone fall for you whom you know is not the one, especially if you have already identified that you are not equally yoked with this person. DO NOT block the path for someone who may be for you!

If you are in a ministry leadership role, you are responsible for setting an example. This is not just about you, but it is about the kingdom. There are others watching how you live this life. Others coming behind you and possibly looking up to you. If you are in ten relationships within ten months, be careful about how you are choosing someone to date. Dating or collecting data is alright but there are some questions and some actions that will, right away, let you know if this is for you. It is alright to ask these questions early.

As a minister of the Gospel, I have noticed that the closer I get to God and the more I focus on the things of Christ, the better I feel and the more confident I am in God. As I discuss the oil in my lamp, I relate it to the anointing on my life. The presence of the Holy Spirit within me. This is definitely not anything that I want to lose or tamper with in any way. I have come to know the power of the Anointing and the necessity for the presence of the Holy Spirit in my life. The oil in my lamp must be protected. It must be guarded.

In other words, I must keep my anointing by being obedient to the call of God in every way possible. I must stay aligned with the Word of God. I must walk after the Spirit and not the flesh. I cannot and will not allow myself to be distracted knowing that the purpose of this life is to please God, not man or myself. So, I say, let the Holy Spirit guide your lives. Then you won't be doing what your sinful nature craves. -Gal 5:16

With that being said, a child of Christ must stay away from an ungodly life. A child of Christ must make correct decisions and love God more than wanting a mate, while single. A true Christian must remember to keep Christ first and refrain from ungodly ways.

Scriptural Guidance:

Psalm 37:4-5 (NIV) *Delight yourself in the LORD, and he will give you the desires of your heart. Commit your way to the LORD; trust in him, and he will act.*

Galatians 5:16 (NIV) *So, I say, let the Holy Spirit guide your lives. Then you won't be doing what your sinful nature craves." -*

Kingdom Focused Activities:

- **Daily Prayer and Meditation:** Spending intentional time in prayer, listening to God, and meditating on Scripture to maintain spiritual alignment.
- **Scripture Journaling:** Reflecting on key Bible verses that encourage trusting God, healing, and restoring relationships.

135

- **Fasting for Clarity and Strength:** Fasting to seek God's direction and healing in specific areas, particularly in waiting and dating.
- **Listening to Worship Music:** Creating an atmosphere of worship, inviting the Holy Spirit to minister and guide you through daily decisions.
- **Reading Christian Books on Relationships and Healing:** Strengthening understanding of God's principles for healthy relationships and the power of His healing.

Forty-Five

DAY 40: A Servant's Heart

1 Peter 4:10 (ESV) Each has received a gift, use it to serve one another, as good stewards of God's varied grace.

Acts 20:35 (NIV) In all things I have shown you that by working hard in this way we must help the weak and remember the words of the Lord Jesus, how he himself said, "It is more blessed to give than to receive."

Matthew 20:28 (NIV) Even as the Son of Man came not to be served but to serve, and to give his life as a ransom for many."

My Understanding of This Journey

Being in ministry and serving God is a profound calling that demands a heart fully dedicated to His divine will. It is a path filled with opportunities to witness the miracles of God's love and grace in the lives of others. In this sacred journey, I become a vessel through which God's mercy flows, bringing light to those in darkness and hope to the weary. It is a privilege and an honor to serve the Almighty, knowing that every act of kindness, every word of encouragement, and every prayer offered in faith can make an eternal impact.

Joy is a cornerstone of my Christian life and an indispensable part of serving in ministry. It is not a fleeting emotion but a deep-seated sense of contentment and happiness that comes from knowing and loving God. This joy sustains me through trials and tribulations, reminding me of the eternal promises of my Heavenly Father. As I minister to others, I share this joy, offering a glimpse of the divine happiness that transcends all earthly struggles. It is this joy that attracts others to the faith, showcasing the transformative power of a life devoted to God. Peace and kindness are the hallmarks of my life in ministry. Peace, which surpasses all understanding, fills my heart as I trust in God's plan and relinquish my worries to Him.

Lesson Learned

It enables me to be calm in the face of adversity and to spread tranquility to those around me. Kindness, on the other hand, is the practical expression of my faith. Through acts of love and compassion, I reflect the character of Christ to the world. Every smile, every helping hand, and every word of comfort speaks volumes about the nature of our God. Together, peace and kindness create a powerful testimony of a life transformed by God's love.

Reflection

Self-reflection is an essential practice for me in ministry, for it is through introspection that I align my heart with God's will. In moments of quiet contemplation, I seek to understand my motivations, to purify my intentions, and to ensure that my service is not for personal glory but for the glory of God. This process allows me to grow spiritually, to identify areas where I fall short, and to humbly ask for God's guidance and strength. By examining my relationship with God, I remain grounded and focused on the true purpose of my ministry.

Prayer

Heavenly Father, I come before You with a heart open to serving others and glorifying Your name. Your Word in 1 Peter 4:10 reminds us, "As each has received a gift, use it to serve one another, as good stewards of God's varied grace." Lord, thank You for the unique gifts and talents You have bestowed upon me. Help me to use these gifts to serve others, being a faithful steward of Your grace.

Acts 20:35 teaches us, "In all things I have shown you that by working hard in this way we must help the weak and remember the words of the Lord Jesus, how he himself said, 'It is more blessed to give than to receive.'" Lord, instill in me a heart of generosity and compassion. May I always remember the blessing of giving and be diligent in helping those who are weak and in need.

In Matthew 20:28, we are reminded that "Even as the Son of Man came not to be served but to serve, and to give his life as a ransom for many." Lord, let the example of Jesus be my guide. Teach me to serve selflessly, putting the needs of others before my own. Help me to follow in the footsteps of Christ, who gave His life as the ultimate act of service and love.

As I navigate my journey of singleness, Lord, I ask for Your guidance and strength. May my life be a reflection of Your love and service. Use me in whatever way You see fit to bring glory to Your name and to advance Your kingdom. Let my singleness be a time of devoted service to You and to those around me.

In Jesus' name, I pray. Amen.

Forty-Six

DAY 41: Surrender it to God

M ark 10:45 (NIV) For even the Son of Man came not to be served but to serve, and to give his life as a ransom for many.

1 Peter 4:10 (NIV) As each has received a gift, use it to serve one another, as good stewards of God's varied grace.

My Understanding of This Journey

The bible reminds that we are called to freedom. Only use your freedom as an opportunity to love and serve one another. As a minister, I find immense joy in the privilege of serving others. Each day, I am reminded of the profound calling to be God's hands and feet in this world, reflecting His love and compassion in everything I do. The joy that comes from witnessing lives transformed by God's grace is unparalleled. It fills my heart with gratitude and inspires me to continue this sacred journey with enthusiasm and dedication. Serving others allows me to experience the fullness of God's love, and it is an honor to be part of His divine plan.

I strive to understand and share in the emotions and struggles of those I serve. When I offer a listening ear or a comforting word, I aim to mirror the empathy and kindness of Christ. My heart aches for those in pain, and I seek to provide solace and support. Through acts of sympathy, I am reminded of Jesus' compassion for the suffering, and it deepens my commitment to minister with a heart full of love and care and that as the word said in 1 Peter 4:10, "As each has received a gift, use it to serve one another, as good stewards of God's varied grace."

Joy permeates my service as I witness the impact of God's work in the lives of others. There is a profound sense of fulfillment in knowing that I can be an instrument of His peace and love. Each act of service, no matter how small, brings me closer to understanding the boundless joy that comes from living a life dedicated to God's will. This joy is contagious, spreading hope and light to those I encounter. It fuels my passion for ministry, encouraging me to serve with an ever-joyful spirit.

Lesson Learned

Being a minister is a godly calling that shapes every aspect of my life. It requires a heart fully surrendered to God's will and a commitment to living out His teachings. I am constantly reminded of the importance of humility, love, and perseverance in my service. Through prayer and reflection, I seek God's guidance and strength to fulfill my calling faithfully. My relationship with Him is the foundation of my ministry, and it is through His grace that I am able to serve others effectively. Each day, I am grateful for the opportunity to walk this path, knowing that I am fulfilling a divine purpose.

Reflection

How can I communicate my faith and values effectively to potential partners without coming across as judgmental or imposing? What specific boundaries do I need to establish in my dating life to maintain integrity in my role as a pastor?

Prayer

Heavenly Father, I humbly come before You, acknowledging the example set by Your Son, Jesus Christ, who came not to be served but to serve. Thank You for the precious gift of salvation He offered through His sacrificial love, giving His life as a ransom for many. As I reflect on His selfless example, I am reminded of the call in 1 Peter 4:10 to use the gifts You have bestowed upon me to serve others.

Lord, I recognize that each of us has received unique gifts and talents from Your hand, and I pray for the wisdom to steward them well for Your glory. Help me to discern how I can best use these gifts to serve those around me, to be a source of encouragement, support, and love to others in need. May I emulate the servant-hearted nature of Jesus, finding joy and fulfillment in selflessly giving of myself for the benefit of others.

Grant me a heart that is eager to serve, Lord, and open my eyes to the opportunities You place before me each day. Whether it be through acts of kindness, words of encouragement, or sharing Your love in tangible ways, may I faithfully fulfill my role as a steward of Your grace. May my life be a reflection of Your love and compassion, drawing others into a deeper relationship with You.

In Jesus' name. Amen.

Forty-Seven

DAY 42: Acceptance

~⊶⊷⊶~

Romans 14:8 (ESV) For if we live, we live to the Lord, and if we die, we die to the Lord. So then, whether we live or whether we die, we are the Lord's.

John 14:1-3 (ESV) Let not your hearts be troubled. Believe in God; believe also in me. In my Father's house are many rooms. If it were not so, would I have told you that I go to prepare a place for you? And if I go and prepare a place for you, I will come again and will take you to myself, that where I am you may be also.

1 Thessalonians 4:13-18 (ESV) But we do not want you to be uninformed, brothers, about those who are asleep, that you may not grieve as others do who have no hope. For since we believe that Jesus died and rose again, even so, through Jesus, God will bring with him those who have fallen asleep. For this we declare to you by a word from the Lord, that we who are alive, who are left until the coming of the Lord, will not precede those who have fallen asleep. For the Lord himself will descend from heaven with a cry of command, with the voice of an archangel, and with the sound of the trumpet of God. And the dead in Christ will rise first. Then we who are alive, who are left, will be caught up together with them in the clouds to meet the Lord in the air, and so we will always be with the Lord.

My Understanding of This Journey

John 14:1-3 "Let not your hearts be troubled. Believe in God; believe also in me. In my father's house are many rooms. If it were not so, would I have told you that I go to prepare a place for you? And if I go and prepare a place for you, I will come again and will take you to myself, that where I am you may be also." Divorce or separation not only marks the end of a relationship but also the loss of the potential and dreams I had for my spouse. I reflect on the hopes, aspirations, and expectations I had for my partner and our life together. I allow myself to acknowledge the disappointment and sadness that comes with realizing these dreams may not come to fruition. I write about the moments of realization and acceptance as I come to terms with the end of this chapter in my life.

Romans 14:8 "For if we live, we live to the Lord, and if we die, we die to the Lord. So then, whether we live or whether we die, we are the Lord's." I consider the ways in which I can find closure and peace amidst the loss of the potential in my spouse. This might involve reframing my perspective, focusing on gratitude for the memories and experiences shared, or finding meaning and purpose in my newfound independence. I reflect on the lessons I learn about resilience, adaptability, and the unpredictability of life. I write about the moments of clarity and insight that emerge as I release the attachment to the future I once imagined.

Lesson Learned

I think about the support systems and resources available to me as I navigate through this aspect of grief. I reflect on the importance of self-compassion and forgiveness as I let go of expectations and embrace the present moment. I consider how practicing mindfulness, and acceptance can help me find peace and fulfillment in the midst of uncertainty. I write about the ways in which I cultivate resilience and strength as I grieve the loss of the potential in my spouse. By documenting these reflections, I honor the complexity of my emotions and the depth of my experience as I navigate through this challenging time.

Reflection

Grieving the loss of the potential in your spouse can be a challenging aspect of divorce or separation. How do you navigate through this process? What strategies help you find closure and acceptance? Write about your feelings and experiences as you grieve the loss of the future you envisioned with your spouse.

Prayer

Heavenly Father, I come before You with a heart full of faith and trust in Your promises. Your Word in Romans 14:8 reminds us that if we live, we live to the Lord, and if we die, we die to the Lord. So then, whether we live or whether we die, we are Yours, Lord. Help me to live each day with this truth in my heart, knowing that my life and my death are in Your hands.

In John 14:1-3, You comfort us by saying, "Let not your hearts be troubled. Believe in God; believe also in me. In my Father's house are many rooms. If it were not so, would I have told you that I go to prepare a place for you? And if I go and prepare a place for you, I will come again and will take you to myself, that where I am you may be also." Lord, thank You for this assurance. Help me to hold on to this promise, especially in times of uncertainty and fear. Let my heart not be troubled but filled with faith in Your preparation for me.

1 Thessalonians 4:13-18 reminds us not to grieve as those who have no hope, for we believe that Jesus died and rose again. Through Jesus, You will bring with You those who have fallen asleep. We are reassured that the Lord Himself will descend from heaven with a cry of command, with the voice of an archangel, and with the sound of the trumpet of God. The dead in Christ will rise first, and then those who are alive will be caught up together with them in the clouds to meet the Lord in the air, and we will always be with the Lord. Lord, thank You for this glorious hope of resurrection and eternal life with You.

Father, I pray for the strength and courage to live each day in the light of these truths. Help me to be a source of comfort and hope to others, sharing the assurance of Your promises. Let my life reflect the hope and joy of knowing that we are Yours, both in life and in death.

In Jesus' name, I pray. Amen.

Forty-Eight

DAY 43: Walking in Purpose

E phesians 6:7 **(NIV)** Rendering service with a good will as to the Lord and not to man.

Joshua 24:15 (NIV) And if it is evil in your eyes to serve the Lord, choose this day whom you will serve, whether the gods your fathers served in the region beyond the River, or the gods of the Amorites in whose land you dwell. But as for me and my house, we will serve the Lord."

Hebrews 6:10 (ESV) For God is not unjust so as to overlook your work and the love that you have shown for his name in serving the saints, as you still do.

My Understanding of This Journey

Walking in my purpose is a journey that fills my heart with joy and peace, knowing that I am aligned with God's will for my life. Each day, I seek to understand more deeply the unique calling that God has placed on my heart. How can I serve Him better today than I did yesterday? What specific gifts has He given me to fulfill this purpose? These questions guide my reflections and help me stay focused on the path He has set before me. By walking in my purpose, I find a profound sense of fulfillment and a steady peace that comes from trusting in His plan.

As I reflect on my journey, I often ask myself how I can be a better steward of the talents and opportunities God has given me. Am I using my time wisely? Are my actions reflecting His love and grace to those around me? These questions keep me grounded and help me evaluate whether I am truly walking in my God-given purpose. Through prayer and meditation, I seek God's guidance, asking Him to reveal any areas where I need growth or redirection. This continuous self-reflection ensures that my steps are always aligned with His divine will.

Walking in my purpose also brings immense joy as I witness the positive impact of my actions on others. It is a joy that transcends circumstances, rooted in the knowledge that I am contributing to something far greater than myself. How can I bring joy to someone else's life today? What acts of kindness and service can I offer that reflect God's love?

Lesson Learned

These questions inspire me to live each day with intentionality and compassion, spreading joy wherever I go. The joy of walking in my purpose is a testament to the beauty of living a life dedicated to serving God and others. Finally, the peace that comes from walking in my purpose is a profound and sustaining force. It is a peace that reassures me even in times of uncertainty, reminding me that I am held in God's hands. This peace is a constant reminder of God's faithfulness and the perfect plans He has for my life.

Reflection

How can you cultivate a deeper sense of peace in my daily walk? Are there areas of my life where I need to surrender more fully to God's will? How can I cultivate a deeper sense of peace in my daily walk? Are there areas of my life where I need to surrender more fully to God's will? By addressing these questions, I can continually deepen my trust in God and embrace the peace that comes from knowing I am exactly where He wants me to be.

Prayer

Heavenly Father, I come before You with gratitude in my heart, knowing that You are a just and loving God who sees and values every act of service done in Your name. Your Word in Ephesians 6:7 instructs us to render service with a good will as to the Lord and not to man. Lord, help me to serve with a heart full of joy and dedication, always remembering that my ultimate service is to You and not to people. May my efforts be pleasing in Your sight and bring honor to Your name.

Joshua 24:15 reminds us to choose whom we will serve, declaring, "But as for me and my house, we will serve the Lord." Father, I choose You. I commit myself and my household to serve You wholeheartedly. Help us to stand firm in our faith, regardless of the challenges we face. May our service be a testament to our love and devotion to You.

In Hebrews 6:10, we are assured that "For God is not unjust so as to overlook your work and the love that you have shown for His name in serving the saints, as you still do." Thank You, Lord, for recognizing the love and labor I pour into serving Your people. Thank You for not overlooking the sacrifices I make for Your kingdom. Give me strength and endurance to continue serving faithfully, knowing that my efforts are not in vain but are pleasing in Your sight.

May my service be a reflection of Your love and grace, drawing others closer to You and bringing glory to Your name.

In Jesus' name, I pray. Amen.

Forty-Nine

DAY 44: Examine Yourself

Galatians 6:9 (NIV) And let us not grow weary of doing good, for in due season we will reap, if we do not give up.

Hebrews 13:16 (NIV) Do not neglect to do good and to share what you have, for such sacrifices are pleasing to God.

Hebrews 6:10 (NIV) For God is not unjust so as to overlook your work and the love that you have shown for his name in serving the saints, as you still do.

My Understanding of This Journey

As a minister for God, I embrace the calling to live with integrity, fully aware that I am held to a higher standard. It is a profound joy to know that my life can reflect the values and teachings of Christ to those around me. Integrity means aligning my actions with my words, ensuring that my daily conduct is a testament to the faith I proclaim. How can I demonstrate integrity in all my interactions today? Am I living in a way that truly reflects the principles I teach? These questions guide me to act with honesty, transparency, and consistency, fostering trust and respect within my community.

Living with integrity as a minister requires a deep commitment to kindness. Every interaction is an opportunity to show the love of Christ through my words and actions. Am I treating others with the respect and compassion they deserve? How can I better serve those in need with kindness and grace? By reflecting on these questions, I strive to embody the kindness that Jesus showed to everyone He met. Whether it's offering a listening ear, a helping hand, or a word of encouragement, I seek to be a source of God's love and grace to all I encounter.

The joy of living with integrity comes from knowing that I am walking in alignment with God's will. There is a profound sense of peace and satisfaction in being true to my beliefs and values, even when it is challenging. How can I maintain my integrity in difficult situations? What steps can I take to ensure that my decisions are rooted in prayer and reflection? These reflections help me stay grounded and committed to doing what is right, regardless of the circumstances. It is this steadfastness that brings joy, knowing that I am fulfilling my calling with honor and faithfulness.

Lesson Learned

I understand that being held to a higher standard is not a burden but a blessing. It is an opportunity to lead by example and inspire others to live lives of integrity and kindness. By living with integrity, I hope to encourage others to do the same, creating a ripple effect of goodness and faithfulness that extends far beyond my immediate reach. The joy and fulfillment that come from this calling are immeasurable, knowing that through God's grace, I can make a positive impact in the lives of others.

Reflection

How can I be a role model for those I serve? What can I do to encourage others to uphold the same values? These questions keep me focused on my mission to be a beacon of light in a world that often lacks these values.

Prayer

Heavenly Father, In times of weariness and doubt, I lift my heart to You, knowing that You are my strength and sustenance. Your Word in Galatians 6:9 encourages us to not grow weary of doing good, for in due season we will reap, if we do not give up. Lord, help me to persevere in kindness and generosity, knowing that my efforts are not in vain. Strengthen me to continue doing good, trusting that Your perfect timing will bring forth a harvest of blessings.

Teach me to heed the words of Hebrews 13:16, to not neglect doing good and sharing what I have, for such sacrifices are pleasing to You. May I always be willing to share my blessings and extend a helping hand to those in need. Let my actions reflect Your love and grace, bringing glory to Your name and spreading Your light in a world in need.

Hebrews 6:10 reassures us that You are not unjust to overlook our work and the love we have shown for Your name in serving the saints. Thank You, Lord, for recognizing the love and labor I pour into serving Your people. Give me the endurance to continue serving faithfully, knowing that my sacrifices are pleasing to You. May my life be a testament to Your love and goodness, drawing others closer to You and bringing honor to Your name.

In Jesus' name, I pray. Amen.

Fifty

DAY 45: Intentional Dating

J ohn 14:6 (NIV) Jesus said to him, "I am the way, and the truth, and the life. No one comes to the Father except through me.

1 Timothy 5:8 (NIV) But if anyone does not provide for his relatives, and especially for members of his household, he has denied the faith and is worse than an unbeliever.

Romans 12:2 (NIV) Do not be conformed to this world, but be transformed by the renewal of your mind, that by testing you may discern what is the will of God, what is good and acceptable and perfect.

My Understanding of This Journey

Dating as a pastor while adhering to the standards set forth by God has been a journey filled with valuable lessons. One significant lesson I've learned is the importance of clear communication and transparency from the outset. Being upfront about my faith, values, and the boundaries I adhere to has been crucial in fostering mutual understanding and respect in any potential relationship. It's essential to ensure that both parties are on the same page regarding faith and lifestyle, as this forms the foundation of a healthy, God-centered relationship.

It is a necessity to set boundaries and stick to them. As a pastor, my role extends beyond just my personal life; I'm also a spiritual leader to my congregation. Therefore, maintaining boundaries in my relationships helps me uphold the integrity of my ministry and remain accountable to God and my community. This means being intentional about avoiding situations or behaviors that could compromise my witness or lead others astray. Furthermore, I've learned the significance of seeking guidance and support from fellow believers and mentors. Dating as a pastor comes with its unique challenges and temptations, and having a strong support system of trusted friends and mentors who share my values has been invaluable. They provide accountability, wisdom, and prayer support, helping me navigate the complexities of relationships while staying true to my faith.

Lesson Learned

I've realized the importance of prioritizing my relationship with God above all else. In the busyness of ministry and personal life, it can be easy to neglect spending quality time with God. However, I've learned that cultivating a deep, intimate relationship with Him is essential not only for my own spiritual well-being but also for the health of any romantic relationship I may pursue. Keeping God at the center ensures that my motives, decisions, and actions align with His will, ultimately leading to a more fulfilling and purposeful dating experience.

Reflection

Who are the trusted individuals in my life whom I can turn to for support, accountability, and guidance in my dating journey? How can I prioritize and nurture my relationship with God amidst the demands of ministry and personal life, ensuring that it remains the foundation of all my relationships?

Prayer

Heavenly Father, In the midst of a world that often pulls us in various directions, I come before You seeking transformation. As Jesus said in John

14:6, "I am the way, and the truth, and the life. No one comes to the Father except through me." Help me, Lord, to follow Your way, embrace Your truth, and live the life You have planned for me.

1 Timothy 5:8 reminds us of our duty to provide for our relatives, especially the members of our household. Lord, give me the strength and wisdom to fulfill my responsibilities faithfully, providing for my family in every way possible, and not denying the faith by neglecting those closest to me.

Romans 12:2 calls us to not be conformed to this world, but to be transformed by the renewal of our minds. Grant me discernment, that through testing, I may uncover Your perfect will for my life. Help me to break free from the patterns of this world and to be renewed in my mind by Your Spirit. Guide me in the paths of righteousness, that I may walk in what is good, acceptable, and perfect in Your sight.

May Your Word be my lamp, illuminating the way forward, and may Your Spirit be my guide, leading me into alignment with Your divine purposes. I pray this in the name of Jesus, who is the way, the truth, and the life. Amen.

Fifty-One

DAY 46: Looking Through God's Eyes

Proverbs 18:24 (NIV) A man of many companions may come to ruin, but there is a friend who sticks closer than a brother.

Proverbs 17:17 (NIV) A friend loves at all times, and a brother is born for adversity.

John 15:12-13 (ESV) This is my commandment, that you love one another as I have loved you. Greater love has no one than this, that someone lay down his life for his friends.

Psalm 133:1 (NIV) Behold, how good and pleasant it is when brothers dwell in unity!

My Understanding of This Journey

Serving God alongside my family and friends has been a profound blessing, enriching our lives with kindness, grace, and joy. Together, I discovered the beauty of living out my faith in community, while supporting and encouraging one another on my spiritual journeys. Through acts of kindness and gestures of grace, I experienced the transformative power of God's love in my relationships, deepening our bonds and fostering a sense of unity rooted in Christ. One valuable lesson I've learned is the importance of extending grace to both others and myself. In the midst of all of these imperfections and shortcoming, grace offers me the freedom to acknowledge my humanity while embracing God's unconditional love and forgiveness. I know that I can cultivate a culture of grace within our family and friend circles, we create an environment where authenticity and vulnerability are celebrated, allowing God's redemptive work to shine through our lives.

Additionally, I've discovered the significance of choosing joy in every circumstance. While life may present its share of challenges and trials, joy is not dependent on our external circumstances but rather on our relationship with God. By cultivating a spirit of gratitude and rejoicing in the Lord's faithfulness, I can experience a profound sense of joy that transcends any temporary hardship or adversity.

Lesson Learned

I am serving God alongside my family and friends; I am talking about the family and friends in God who have taught me the beauty of unity in diversity. Each member brings their unique gifts, talents, and perspectives to our shared journey of faith, enriching our experiences and deepening our understanding of God's purposes. Through humility and mutual respect, we embrace our differences and celebrate the richness of God's creation reflected in our relationships.

Reflection

How can I cultivate a culture of grace within my family and friend circles, fostering an environment of forgiveness, acceptance, and love? In what ways can I intentionally choose joy in the midst of challenges and difficulties, trusting in God's sovereignty and faithfulness? How can I honor and appreciate the diverse gifts and perspectives of my family and friends, fostering unity amidst our differences? How can I actively seek opportunities to serve and support my loved ones in their spiritual growth and journey with God?

Prayer

Heavenly Father, Thank You for the gift of family and friends with whom I can serve and journey alongside in faith. Your Word in Proverbs 18:24 reminds us that while many companions may come to ruin, there is a friend who sticks closer than a brother. Lord, help us to be those faithful friends who love at all times, as Proverbs 17:17 teaches, and to support each other through every adversity.

In John 15:12-13, You command us to love one another as You have loved us, and You have shown us that the greatest love is to lay down one's life for friends. Lord, may our love for each other reflect this sacrificial love, growing deeper and stronger every day.

Psalm 133:1 celebrates the goodness and pleasantness of brothers dwelling in unity. Father, grant us the grace to live in unity, embracing the beauty of our diversity and working together to bring glory to Your name.

May Your kindness, grace, and joy abound in our relationships, shaping us into vessels of Your love and instruments of Your peace. Help us to extend grace to one another, to choose joy in all circumstances, and to embrace the beauty of our diversity in unity. Guide us as we seek to serve You together, strengthening our bonds and deepening our commitment to Your kingdom.

In Jesus' name. Amen.

Fifty-Two

DAY 47: Everyone Matters

⟨ornament⟩

J ohn 15:12 (NIV) This is my commandment, that you love one another as I have loved you.

Mark 10:45 (NIV) For even the Son of Man came not to be served but to serve, and to give his life as a ransom for many.

Matthew 23:11 (NIV) The greatest among you shall be your servant.

My Understanding of This Journey

Serving our neighbors in love, in Christ Jesus, has been a cornerstone of my faith journey, revealing the transformative power of kindness and grace. As we heed Christ's call to love our neighbors as ourselves, we become vessels of His love, extending compassion and mercy to those in need. Whether through acts of service, words of encouragement, or simply offering a listening ear, we have the privilege of being instruments of God's love in the lives of those around us. One profound lesson I've learned through serving our neighbors is the importance of humility. In humbly serving others, we emulate the example of Christ, who took on the form of a servant and laid down His life for us. By setting aside our own agendas and preferences, we create space for God's love to flow through us, touching the hearts and lives of those we encounter.

Moreover, I've discovered the power of building relationships based on genuine care and compassion. Beyond meeting physical needs, true transformation occurs when we engage with our neighbors on a personal level, seeking to understand their stories, struggles, and aspirations. Through authentic relationships grounded in Christ's love, we become catalysts for lasting change and restoration in our communities.

Furthermore, serving our neighbors has deepened my appreciation for the diversity of God's creation. Each individual bears the image of God and possesses inherent dignity and worth. By embracing diversity and honoring the unique gifts and contributions of every person, we reflect the beauty of God's kingdom, where all are valued and cherished as beloved children of God.

Reflection

How can I cultivate a spirit of humility in my service to others, recognizing that true greatness is found in sacrificial love? In what ways can I foster genuine relationships with my neighbors, seeking to understand their needs and journeying with them in love and compassion? How can I celebrate and embrace the diversity of my community, honoring the image of God reflected in each individual? What practical steps can I take to continue serving my neighbors with kindness, grace, and Christ-centered love in both word and deed?

Prayer

Heavenly Father, Thank You for the teachings and example of Jesus, who commanded us to love one another as He has loved us, as stated in John 15:12. Help us to embody this love in our daily lives, showing kindness, compassion, and understanding to everyone we encounter.

In Mark 10:45, we are reminded that even the Son of Man came not to be served but to serve and to give His life as a ransom for many. Lord, instill in us a servant's heart, always ready and willing to serve others selflessly, just as

Jesus did. May our actions reflect Your love and bring glory to Your name.

Matthew 23:11 teaches that the greatest among us shall be our servant. Father, grant us the humility to serve others with grace and joy. Let us find greatness in serving and lifting others up, following the path that Jesus laid before us. Guide us in our journey of faith, helping us to love, serve, and honor You in all that we do. May our lives be a testament to Your love and grace.

In Jesus' name. Amen.

Fifty-Three

DAY 48: Understanding God's Love

ebrews 13:16 (ESV) Do not neglect to do good and to share what you have, for such sacrifices are pleasing to God.

Galatians 6:2 (ESV) Bear one another's burdens, and so fulfill the law of Christ.

My Understanding of This Journey

The capacity to love like God, to embrace others with kindness and godly joy, is a journey I've embarked on with both awe and humility. As I strive to reflect the boundless love of our Creator, I've learned that this divine love transcends human understanding, encompassing every soul with compassion and grace. Embracing others with the same love that God extends to us requires a heart transformed by His Spirit, a heart open to the beauty and worth of every individual, regardless of differences or shortcomings.

One profound lesson I've learned in seeking to love like God is the power of forgiveness. Just as God forgives us unconditionally, He calls us to extend that same forgiveness to others. Through forgiveness, we release the burden of resentment and bitterness, making room for healing and reconciliation to take place. By embracing a posture of forgiveness, we reflect the transformative love of God, paving the way for restoration and renewal in our relationships. Furthermore, I've discovered the importance of cultivating a spirit of empathy and compassion. To love like God means to enter into the joys and sorrows of others, bearing their burdens with tenderness and care. When we empathize with the experiences of those around us, we create space for genuine connection and understanding, fostering a community marked by compassion and solidarity.

Lesson Learned

The journey to love like God has taught me the significance of embracing godly joy in every circumstance. Unlike fleeting happiness, godly joy is rooted in the unchanging truth of God's love and promises. It is a deep, abiding sense of contentment and gratitude that transcends outward circumstances, sustaining us through life's trials and tribulations.

Reflection

How can I cultivate a heart of forgiveness, releasing any bitterness or resentment that hinders my capacity to love like God? In what ways can I practice empathy and compassion, entering into the joys and sorrows of others with genuine care and understanding? How can I nurture a spirit of godly joy in my life, anchoring my heart in the unchanging love and promises of God? What steps can I take to continue growing in my capacity to love like God, embracing others with kindness, grace, and joy in both word and deed?

Prayer

Heavenly Father, Thank You for the boundless love You have lavished upon me, enabling me to love others as You have loved me. As Hebrews 13:16 instructs, help me to not neglect doing good and sharing what I have, knowing that such sacrifices are pleasing to You. Guide me to bear one another's burdens, as Galatians 6:2 teaches, fulfilling the law of Christ with compassion and grace.

Grant me the strength and grace to forgive as You forgive, to empathize as You empathize, and to rejoice in Your presence with godly joy. Fill my heart with Your love, that I may embrace others with kindness, grace, and compassion, reflecting Your image to the world. Guide me on this journey of love, that Your kingdom may be known, and Your name glorified. In Jesus' name. Amen.

Fifty-Four

DAY 49: Intimacy with God

~~~ ❧❧❧ ~~~

J ames 4:8 (NIV) Draw near to God, and he will draw near to you. Cleanse your hands, you sinners, and purify your hearts, you double-minded.

Jeremiah 29:11 (ESV) For I know the plans I have for you," declares the Lord, "plans for welfare and not for evil, to give you a future and a hope.

Isaiah 65:24 (ESV) Before they call, I will answer; while they are yet speaking, I will hear.

My Understanding of This Journey

Intimacy with God is the deepest longing of my heart, a desire to know Him more intimately and to walk closely with Him in every aspect of my life. In the stillness of prayer and the pages of Scripture, I have encountered the boundless love and grace of my Heavenly Father, drawing me into a relationship marked by intimacy and vulnerability. Through moments of worship and communion, I have experienced the joy of His presence, filling my soul with a peace that surpasses all understanding. One profound lesson I've learned in cultivating intimacy with God is the importance of prioritizing time spent in His presence. In the busyness of life, it's easy to allow distractions and obligations to take precedence over nurturing my relationship with God. Yet, I've discovered that true intimacy requires intentional investment – carving out moments each day to seek His face, to listen for His voice, and to commune with Him in prayer.

Furthermore, intimacy with God has taught me the transformative power of surrender. In relinquishing control and surrendering my will to His, I've experienced a profound sense of freedom and peace. Surrender is not a sign of weakness but rather a posture of trust and dependence on the One who knows and loves me intimately. Through surrender, I open myself up to God's guidance and direction, allowing Him to lead me into paths of righteousness and abundance.

Lesson Learned

I find a joy that transcends circumstances, a joy rooted in the unchanging character of God. That is only when I stay connected with God. It is this joy is not dependent on fleeting pleasures or external validation but is found in the assurance of His love and the hope of eternity. It is a joy that sustains me through life's trials and tribulations, anchoring my soul in His unfailing goodness and grace.

Reflection

How can I prioritize intimacy with God in my daily life, making time for prayer, meditation, and reflection on His Word? In what areas of my life do I struggle to surrender control to God, and how can I cultivate a deeper sense of trust and dependence on Him? What brings me true joy and contentment, and how can I nurture a deeper sense of joy in my relationship with God? How does intimacy with God shape my perspective on life's challenges and uncertainties, and how can I lean into His presence for peace and guidance?

Prayer

Heavenly Father, I thank You for the gift of intimacy with You, for the privilege of knowing You more deeply each day. Your Word promises in

James 4:8, "Draw near to God, and he will draw near to you. Cleanse your hands, you sinners, and purify your hearts, you double-minded." Help me to prioritize my relationship with You above all else, carving out sacred moments to seek Your face and hear Your voice.

Lord, I am comforted by Your promise in Jeremiah 29:11, "For I know the plans I have for you," declares the Lord, "plans for welfare and not for evil, to give you a future and a hope." Teach me the beauty of surrender, that I may trust You completely and follow Your leading in every area of my life.

Your Word in Isaiah 65:24 reassures me, "Before they call, I will answer; while they are yet speaking, I will hear." Fill me with Your joy and peace, Lord, anchoring my soul in Your unfailing love. I trust in Your perfect plans for my life, knowing that You hear my prayers and are always with me.

In Your precious name, Amen.

Fifty-Five

DAY 50: Quality Time with God

Jeremiah 33:3 (NIV) Call to me and I will answer you and will tell you great and hidden things that you have not known.

2 Chronicles 6:18 (NIV) But will God indeed dwell with mankind on the earth? Behold, heaven and the highest heaven cannot contain You; how much less this house which I have built.

Deuteronomy 4:39 (NIV) Know therefore today, and take it to your heart, that the Lord, He is God in heaven above and on the earth below; there is no other.

My Understanding of This Journey

God is here, His presence a constant comfort and assurance amid life's busyness and challenges. Each day, I make it a priority to spend time with Him, setting aside moments of quiet reflection and prayer to draw near to His heart. In these sacred moments, I feel His presence enveloping me with love and grace, filling me with a deep sense of peace and joy that transcends all understanding. Whether in the quiet solitude of the early morning or the stillness of the evening, I cherish these precious moments spent in communion with my Heavenly Father.

As I spend daily time with God, His love and kindness overflow within me, prompting me to extend the same love and kindness to those around me. His love becomes a wellspring of compassion, inspiring acts of generosity and selflessness towards others. In His presence, I am reminded of the profound truth that we are called to love one another as He has loved us, embodying His love in tangible ways that bring healing and restoration to a broken world.

Lesson Learned

Spending daily time with God fills my heart with a deep sense of peace and joy that surpasses all understanding. In His presence, I find refuge from the storms of life, anchoring my soul in His unchanging goodness and faithfulness. This peace guards my heart and mind, even during uncertainty and turmoil, reminding me that He is always with me, guiding me with His steadfast love.

Reflection

How can I make daily time with God a consistent priority in my life, setting aside intentional moments for prayer, meditation, and reflection on His Word? In what ways can I extend God's love and kindness to those around me, embodying His compassion and generosity in my interactions with others? How does spending daily time with God cultivate a deep sense of peace and joy within me, and how can I share that peace and joy with others who may be in need?

Prayer

Heavenly Father, I come before You with a heart full of gratitude and love. Your Word in 1 John 4:19 reminds us that we love because You first loved us. Lord, thank You for Your unending love, which serves as the foundation of our lives. Help me to love others as You have loved me, showing kindness and compassion in all my interactions.

Galatians 5:22-23 teaches us that the Holy Spirit produces this kind of fruit in our lives: love, joy, peace, patience, kindness, goodness, faithfulness, gentleness, and self-control. Lord, I pray that these fruits will flourish in my life. Fill me with Your Spirit so that I may exhibit love, joy, and peace in abundance. Grant me patience and kindness in dealing with others, and help me to live a life of goodness, faithfulness, gentleness, and self-control.

In 2 Timothy 1:7, You remind us that You have not given us a spirit of fear and timidity, but of power, love, and self-discipline. Lord, strengthen me with Your power and love. Remove any fear or timidity from my heart and fill me with courage and self-discipline. Let Your Spirit guide me in all that I do, empowering me to live boldly for You.

Thank You, Father, for Your love and for the gifts of the Holy Spirit. Help me to live a life that reflects Your love and brings glory to Your name.

In Jesus' name, I pray. Amen.

Fifty-Six

DAY 51: Love Perfected

1 **John 4:8 (ESV)** But anyone who does not love does not know God, for God is love.

1 **John 4:16 (ESV)** We know how much God loves us, and we have put our trust in his love. God is love, and all who live in love live in God, and God lives in them.

John 3:16 (ESV) For God so loved the world, that he gave his only begotten Son, that whosoever believeth in him should not perish, but have everlasting life.

My Understanding of This Journey

God is love, and His love is the guiding force that shapes my interactions with others. As I strive to love like God, I am reminded that love is not merely a feeling but a choice and a commitment to extend kindness, joy, and peace to all whom I encounter. His love compels me to see each person through His eyes, recognizing their inherent worth and treating them with dignity and respect. Loving like God means embodying kindness in all my words and actions and seeking opportunities to uplift and encourage those around me. Whether through a simple act of compassion or a heartfelt word of encouragement, I endeavor to spread His love wherever I go, knowing that even the smallest gestures can make a significant difference in someone's life.

Lesson Learned

I love God because He fills my heart with a deep sense of joy and peace that transcends circumstances. In His love, I find a source of unshakeable joy rooted in the knowledge that I am deeply loved and cherished by my Heavenly Father. This joy sustains me through life's trials and challenges, anchoring my soul in His unfailing goodness and grace.

Reflection

How can I love like God in practical ways, embodying kindness, joy, and peace in my interactions with others? What barriers or challenges do I face in loving like God, and how can I overcome them with His help? How does experiencing God's love for me deepen my capacity to love others, and how can I share that love with those who need it most?

Prayer

Dear Heavenly Father, Thank You for the gift of Your boundless love. Your Word reminds us that anyone who does not love does not know You, for You are love (1 John 4:8). Help me to truly know You by living in love. I am grateful for Your love that abides in me and empowers me to love others. Your love is perfect and transformative, and I ask that You help me to trust in it fully (1 John 4:16).

Lord, I am in awe of the love You showed by giving Your only begotten Son, Jesus Christ, so that I might have eternal life (John 3:16). Let this amazing love guide me in all I do. Fill my heart with Your Holy Spirit, removing any barriers that hinder my capacity to love as You do. May my life reflect Your love, extending kindness, joy, and peace to everyone I encounter.

Thank You for Your everlasting love. In Jesus' name, Amen.

Fifty-Seven

DAY 52: Testimony and Worship

Heavenly Father, I come before You with a heart overflowing with gratitude for the testimony You've written in my life. You've guided me through valleys of uncertainty and led me to mountaintops of triumph, showing Your faithfulness every step of the way. As a single pastor, I've witnessed Your handiwork in my ministry and personal journey, and I am humbled by Your relentless pursuit of my heart. Lord, may my testimony be a beacon of hope and encouragement to others, pointing them towards Your unfailing love and grace. Grant me the courage and boldness to share Your faithfulness with those who need to hear it, that Your name may be glorified in all I do.

Gracious God, in the stillness of this moment, I quiet my heart to listen for Your voice. As a single pastor navigating the complexities of life and ministry, I long to hear Your guidance and direction. Speak to me, Lord, in whispers of assurance and clarity, that I may walk in obedience to Your will. Open my ears to discern Your voice amidst the noise of the world, and grant me the wisdom to follow where You lead. May every decision I make be rooted in Your truth and aligned with Your purposes. In Your presence, I find strength and confidence, knowing that You are with me every step of the way. In Jesus name, Amen.

Precious Father, as a single pastor serving in Your vineyard, I am reminded of the privilege and responsibility of bearing witness to Your love and grace. You've entrusted me with the sacred task of shepherding Your flock, and I am grateful for the opportunity to proclaim Your goodness to those in my care. Lord, ignite a fire within me to passionately pursue Your presence and seek Your face daily. Renew my spirit and revive my passion for Your kingdom work so that I may serve You wholeheartedly and lead others into deeper intimacy with You. May my life be a living testimony to Your transformative power, drawing others into Your loving embrace. In Jesus name, Amen.

Heavenly Father, as I reflect on Your faithfulness in my life as a single pastor, my heart overflows with gratitude and praise. You've shown me time and again that You are a God who hears and answers prayers, and I am in awe of Your unfailing love. Lord, in the moments of doubt and uncertainty, remind me of Your promises and reassure me of Your presence. Help me to trust in Your perfect timing and to lean on Your understanding when the path ahead seems unclear. As I continue to seek Your guidance and direction, may Your voice be the loudest one I hear, leading me in paths of righteousness for Your name's sake. In Jesus name, Amen.

Verses for Reflection:

- **Galatians 5:13 (ESV)** For you were called to freedom, brothers. Only do not use your freedom as an opportunity for the flesh, but through love serve one another.
- **Romans 12:11 (ESV)** Do not be slothful in zeal, be fervent in spirit, serve the Lord.
- **1 Peter 4:10 (ESV)** As each has received a gift, use it to serve one another, as good stewards of God's varied grace.
- **Acts 20:35 (ESV)** In all things I have shown you that by working hard in this way we must help the weak and remember the words of the Lord Jesus, how he himself said, "It is more blessed to give than to receive."
- **Matthew 20:28 (ESV)** Even as the Son of Man came not to be served but to serve, and to give his life as a ransom for many.

- **Hebrews 13:16 (ESV)** Do not neglect to do good and to share what you have, for such sacrifices are pleasing to God.
- **Galatians 6:2 (ESV)** Bear one another's burdens, and so fulfill the law of Christ.

Self-Reflection and Emotional Healing Activities

- **Writing Letters to God:** Expressing your emotions, frustrations, desires, and questions in letter form to God to unburden your heart and seek guidance.
- **Gratitude Journaling:** Focusing on the blessings in your life, even during waiting or challenging times, to cultivate a positive mindset.
- **Forgiveness Exercises:** Actively forgiving past hurts or toxic relationships by releasing them in prayer, symbolically writing them down, and destroying the paper.
- **Therapeutic Counseling or Christian Counseling:** Seeking professional help to heal from emotional wounds or unhealthy patterns in past relationships.

Engaging in Faith-Building Community Activities

- **Joining a Bible Study Group or Small Group:** Engaging in fellowship with others who are also seeking to align their lives with God's will.
- **Attending Church or Worship Services Regularly:** Staying connected to a faith-based community to keep growing spiritually.
- **Volunteering in Ministry:** Serving others can be a way to focus on God's purpose and find healing through giving.
- **Attending Christian Conferences or Retreats:** Dedicating time to hear from spiritual leaders and engaging in corporate worship with a focus on healing and anointing.

Physical and Mental Well-being Activities

- **Exercise and Physical Health Practices:** Keeping your body active with workouts or activities you enjoy (like walking, yoga, or swimming) to maintain balance.
- **Healthy Eating and Cooking Activities:** Preparing nourishing meals that support not only physical health but emotional and spiritual health as a discipline of caring for the body God gave you.
- **Practicing Sabbath Rest:** Taking intentional time away from daily tasks to rest and focus on God's healing and renewal.

Creative and Relational Restoration Activities

- **Creative Expression (Art, Writing, Music):** Expressing feelings through creative outlets to release tension and find emotional healing.
- **Nature Walks or Outdoor Retreats:** Spending time in nature, connecting with God's creation as a form of restoration and peace.
- **Purposeful Dating or Courtship Guided by Biblical Principles:** If in a dating season, pursuing relationships that honor God, with boundaries and intentional communication.

Anointing and Spiritual Empowerment Activities

- **Anointing Oil Prayers:** Using anointing oil in personal prayer times, symbolizes the covering of the Holy Spirit in your life and relationships.
- **Spiritual Warfare Prayers:** Engaging in prayer against spiritual attacks, distractions, and emotional baggage that can affect your walk with God.
- **Speaking in Tongues (if applicable):** Using spiritual gifts like speaking in tongues to deepen your prayer life and connection with the Holy Spirit.

Fifty-Eight

Conclusion

The Journey to Kingdom Focus

As you conclude this 52-day journey, I hope you have experienced God's deep love, guidance, and presence in new and powerful ways. These past weeks have been filled with opportunities to realign your heart, mind, and spirit with God's purpose. As you've navigated the reflections, Scriptures, and prayers, I trust that God has spoken to you, drawing you closer to Him and helping you recognize areas where He is calling you to grow.

The Bible reminds us in **Matthew 6:33**, "Seek first the Kingdom of God and His righteousness, and all these things will be added to you." This journal has been a tool to remind you that everything we do, think, and plan should revolve around the Kingdom of God. Life can be full of distractions, but staying Kingdom-focused ensures that we walk in His will, fulfilling the purpose He has destined for us.

Throughout this journey, remember that **you are anointed, called, and set apart**. Protect the oil in your lamp—stay close to God through prayer, His Word, and obedience to His voice. As you move forward, stay vigilant in guarding your anointing, pursuing His presence, and walking in love.

You have a unique role to play in advancing God's Kingdom, and every step of obedience brings glory to Him.

Afterword

Dear Reader,

As you close this chapter of your spiritual journey, know that **you are loved beyond measure**. God's love for you is everlasting and constant, no matter where you are or what you've experienced. There may have been days during this journal when you felt overwhelmed, or perhaps you felt renewed and empowered. In every season, God has been walking with you, gently guiding your heart and holding your hand.

I want to encourage you to stay focused on the Kingdom. There is no greater calling than serving God and living out His purpose for your life. Be patient in the process and trust that He is working everything out for your good. Remember that **you are never alone**. God's presence is with you every day, filling you with peace and strength to navigate whatever comes your way.

As you continue forward, stay committed to seeking God's heart, guarding your anointing, and living a life that reflects His love. Let His Kingdom be your priority, and watch as He opens doors, restores your soul, and fills your life with His abundant grace.

You are loved, cherished, and called for such a time as this. Keep your eyes fixed on Jesus, and never forget the power of walking in His love and truth.

With love and blessings,

Love you all

The New Kingdom Focused Family

About the Author

Jacqueline Taji Gilchrist is a psychotherapist, professional speaker, author, and founder of New Kingdom Focused Global Ministries. With over 20 years of experience in counseling and leadership, she specializes in mental health, substance abuse, and organizational development, particularly serving underserved communities. She holds a Master's Degree in clinical psychology from Fisk University and a Master's in Divinity with a focus on Pastoral Counseling from Liberty University.

As the founder of JGilchrist Consulting LLC, Jacqueline offers executive-level life counseling, spiritual guidance, and staff development services. She is also the author of Bootcamp for Love: 30 Days to Renewed Relationships and is passionate about helping individuals overcome their mental, emotional, and spiritual challenges to live with purpose.

Dr. Chimene Castor holds a Ph.D. in Nutritional Sciences and is a passionate advocate for global nutrition and wellness. She has participated in church missions to Kenya and South Africa, promoting nutritional health and well-being. Deeply rooted in her faith, Dr. Castor actively serves her community by leading life groups, supporting the children's ministry, and co-founding the New Kingdom Focused/Marriage Ministry. She is also the founder of Sowing Seeds Inc., a non-profit dedicated to advancing nutrition and education in Haiti and Kenya, and the owner of Complete Nutrition Therapy and Counseling, LLC, and Julio Rameaux Farm, LLC. Through her businesses, she emphasizes plant-based approaches to combat chronic diseases and supports sustainable health solutions globally.

Cajuana Capps is a certified project manager professional and a leader in Information Technology and Finance at the University of California, San Diego. An entrepreneur and Christian spiritual leader, she is passionate about living a life of freedom and purpose through her deep relationship with Jesus Christ. Cajuana's mission is to teach others to live with love, compassion, and empowerment by embracing the gift of everlasting freedom. She enjoys Bible study, traveling, and spending time with her family.

Contributing Authors

Natassja Allen is a dedicated woman of God and a graduate of Fiorello H. LaGuardia High School of Music and Art & Performing Arts. She is not only a talented vocalist but also the founder of No More Secrets Inc., a nonprofit dedicated to supporting survivors of domestic violence in the church. Additionally, she is the CEO of Naturally Classy Adornments LLC, a natural skincare and herbal medicine company, where she uses her skills as a certified herbalist to promote healing through nature. Natassja is the co-founder of New Kingdom Focused/Marriage Ministry. She works well with others and is passionate about helping those in need.

Tracey Gooding holds a Master's in Speech and Interpersonal Communication from New York University and a Bachelor's in Speech and Language Pathology from Pace University. She has developed education programs for adolescents and collaborated with various NYC organizations. Tracey is the co-founder of New Kingdom Focused Ministry/Marriage Ministry and is passionate about helping others. In her free time, she enjoys traveling, reading, cooking, and photography. Currently, she is a substitute teacher in Garden City Schools.

Calizza Farrell holds a Master's degree in Business Administration and a Bachelor's degree in Accounting from Northern Illinois University. She has over 15+ years of accounting, business consulting and management experience. She is currently a certified Life Coach, Business Entrepreneur and an Executive Director of a nonprofit. Calizza is a co-founder of New Kingdom Focused Ministry/Marriage Ministry. She enjoys serving her community, reading, fellow-shipping with family and friends and worshiping the Lord.

You can connect with me on:

🅵 https://www.facebook.com/newkingdomfocused

🔗 https://youtube.com/@newkingdomfocused

Made in the USA
Middletown, DE
24 October 2024